the stapled brain

With love to my dear lady wife Frances,
a most fervent and 'Frank' supporter of my contorted
careerings through our many years of fun and frustrations.

the stapled brain
collected writings of Ron Geesin

*For ultimate amusement
handled with care by*

[signature] 2021/04/30

First published in 2020 by
Ron Geesin
Headscope
Street End Lane
Broad Oak
Heathfield
E. Sussex TN21 8TU
UK

www.rongeesin.com

© Ron Geesin 2020

All rights reserved

ISBN : 978-1-8381451-0-1

No part of this publication may be reproduced or transmitted in any form or by any means, electronic or mechanical, including photocopying, recording, or information storage and retrieval system, without permission in writing from Ron Geesin or his legally-appointed representative.

Brain on front cover created by
Frances Geesin in melted polypropylene.
Photographs by Ron Geesin.
Graphic design by Ron Geesin and Dinah Lone.
Final layout by D & N Publishing, Baydon, Wiltshire.

HELLO

Ron as The Consultant

The more I got annoyed by the pedestrian attempts at programming contemporary youth for the materialist machine through my secondary school days at that blushing sandstone edifice of conformity, Hamilton Academy, the more I had to scribble antidotes and annoy the English teachers by playing with words, even creating new ones, in essays.

By the time I was on the road at seventeen-and-a-half with the Original Downtown Syncopators jazz band, I was able to intensify and expand my surreal involvement with surrounding humanity and, in particular, its multi-mental cavortions (contorted cavortings) as it thrashed about dodging the materialistic machine's mincing, and feeding itself. These observations, whether fantastic or truth-revealing, intensified my scribbling in cheap notebooks and on any available loose paper.

Ever since I was sixteen and discovered Freud's 'The Interpretation Of Dreams' in the local Hamilton town library I have been fascinated to observe in myself and others how the human mind shifts ideas, thought patterns, mental notions, up and down the many floors and chambers that comprise its conscious and subconscious in attempt to understand its place in the World and Universe. These observations, sometimes appearing as fixations, form a multi-coloured line running throughout the fabric of this collection – which is fairly complete, less a few unintelligible ramblings where I surpassed myself in writhing convolutions. Mind you, Lewis Carroll converted 'reading and writing' into 'reeling and writhing' – and I well remember lying under a bench along the front of Brodick, Isle of Arran, with my long-lasting friend, artist Bruce McLean, shouting, "Everything is nothing and nothing is everything!" a large empty bottle of cider lying close by. Temper all this with a favourite statement by the wise Chinese philosopher Lin Yutang, "The human brain is but an over-developed food-seeking mechanism".

Since one of my means of tackling the frustrations induced by the Scottish education system was to paint surreal exorcisms, I might have set off in my life after school on an expressive visual path, but certain turns of fortune opened me up to the world of sound, that invisibly mysterious multi-layered medium that is still little understood and often abused. So, striving to understand the invisible may have led me to all this. Somewhat obsessed by form in the expressive arts, I have grouped my 'writhings' into four distinct sections, Noun Clown, Stage Rage, Rhyme Time and Read Right.

The reason I've dated everything as accurately as possible is to satisfy, or frustrate, the modern human's desire to know where and when any creative utterance happened. There is so much mistrust of the inherent ingredients of these manifestations that labels, classifications and stamps of authenticity are frequently required before consumers can give themselves over to actual enjoyment. And, exasperated by the present lack of date conformity, particularly between the UK and the USA, I'm proposing a standard which is logical and suits filing systems and computer databases. In the UK, I'm writing this on the 4th August 2020 (04/08/20) which, in the USA, would be August 4th 2020 (08/04/20). In this book, it's 2020/08/04.

All the early pieces from my *FALLABLES* book ('*ALL FABLES* would have been all wrong'), published in 1975, are included.

Rather like cats who always turn around to examine their shit to find out how they are, artists do 'art' to find out who they are. This is usually an enjoyable occupation, but sometimes a bit of a strain that can lead to fissures – hence the staples. I can give only two final clues to your unpicking of them:

The trouble with me is that I think
I know too many answers!

The sentiments expressed here are not
necessarily those of the Editor.

CONTENTS

section 1

noun clown   **page 14**

An alphabetically arranged set of aphorisms ('short, pithy, witty statements or maxims') and anti-aphorisms (far-from-short mind meanderings). These emerge spasmodically and have been inspired by Rochfoucauld's *'Maxims and Moral Reflections'* and Bierce's *'(Enlarged) Devil's Dictionary'*.

pp. 14–55

Part of a 1968 notebook

section 2: stage rage

page 56

Contains many pieces that were written specifically for my live performances: scripts for monologues to be dramatically delivered from a performing situation which, for me, has included balcony, passageway, dressing-room, toilet, orchestra pit, foyer, the pavement outside, and even a seat amongst the audience. I am stimulated by the extra acoustic and social possibilities from these positions. The pieces vary in styles to suit the content and certainly incorporate methods shown in **noun clown** and **rhyme time**. Should you want to perform them, I have indicated my delivery method where relevant.

On stage at The Third Eye Centre, Glasgow, 1979/09/01

A Bit Of Paper	page 56
A Great Deal Of Mouth	56
A Pleasant Scene	57
A Useful Brick	58
Abuse	58
Add Minister	58
Ailments	60
Alphabite	60
Appearances	61
Barbed Wire	61
Bitter Letters	62
Bloomers	62
Brass Butterfly	62
British Wail	63
Conservation Piece	64
Cubicle	65
Dance	65
Dinner Party	65
Dog-Walk	66
Drugs	66
Enthusiasm	66
Failure	66
Fear The Lord	67
Glasgow – an aspect	68
Give	69
God	69
Grand Search	70
Head Boil	71
Head-Knock	72
Heart	72
Holes	72
Jazz Band	73
Jesus	74
Look	74
Lost And Found	74
Material Miss	75
Nerves	75
Now – more or less	75
Nut	76
On Going	77
Perception	78
Performance – Bracknell, 25th May 1979	78
Pretty Little Faces	79
Pretty Little Girls	80
Rise Up Sebastian	81
Round And Round	83
School Groups – 8.55am	84
Seen	84
Sentence	85
Shipping Water	85
Talking Man	85
The Night Of Nights	86
The Postman Carried A Large Tree	88
The Sound	89
Thought Spot	91
Thought Weave	92
To Be Again Forthcoming With The Second And Third The Next	93
To The Sterile Village Of Bothwell, Lanarkshire	94
Today	95
Train Travellers	96
Turmoil	96
Twist	96
Two Feet And A Mouth	97
Waiting For Life	98
Walking	99
Widdle	99
Wind Of Life	100
Wrong Line	101

section 3

rhyme time

page 102

Self-explanatory. I enjoy diddly-diddly rhythm patterns. They soothe in various ways, like in the accented repetition of children's games, the sub-conscious relaxed swinging of a leg on a train and the manic rocking of a mental patient.

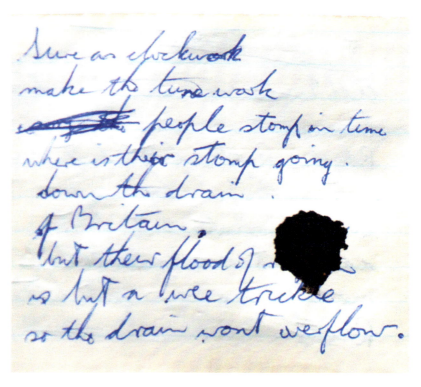

From a 1966 notebook

A Brisk Walk Out	page 102	Mini Liquid Golf Game Thankyou	124
A Revelous Fellow	102	Monks Green Farm (An Imaginary History)	125
A Twisted Tree	102	Nice Old Lady	125
Almost Nearly	103	No Doubt Influenced By Spike Milligan	126
Back Britain	104	Nutcracker Thankyou	127
Bag Of Love	104	O'er Precipice	127
Bath Oil Thankyou	105	On Cooking Roast Pork, Braised Onions & Fresh Runner Beans – With A Bottle Of Red Wine – For The Cook And Author (the same)	128
Bon Fire	105		
Bow-Tie Thankyou	105		
Brain-Twirl	106		
Britain Is Great	107	On Visiting A Middle-Class Aspect	128
By The Sea	107	One Pair Of Eyes	129
Cards Thankyou	107	Oriental Food Thankyou	129
Chrisfarce	108	Page Watcher	130
Confession	110	Patterned Hankies Thankyou	131
Doors	110	Relief	131
Fashion	110	Ron's Address	132
Film	111	Shortbread Thankyou	133
For Katie Hewitt – aged 9	112	Standing Joke	133
For Sale	112	Tartan	134
Geesin's An Odd Name	113	10p Travel Fare	135
Gone – But Nearly There	114	The Pear-Shaped Man	137
Grated Britain	116	The Pen	137
Houses	117	The Well-Appointed Roll	138
I've Never Come This Way Before	118	To A New Couple	138
Jane & Mike Fond Do	120	To Sam Smith	139
Lockdown	121	Two Bottles Bordeaux Thankyou	140
Lying In Bed	121	Two Fellows	140
Man Of Business	122	Unbuilding	141
Message	124	Valentines	141

section 4

read right

page 142

Houses short, and shorter, stories and those pieces that very obviously won't fit anywhere else; quasi-philosophical ponderings and social observations included. Overall, the fact is that several pieces can't fit in any of these sections and will therefore be in the wrong one! This clever technique pulls the whole volume together to become **the stapled brain**.

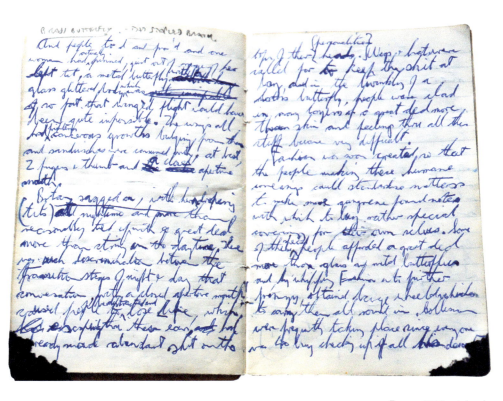

From a 1968 notebook

Alcoholic Intake	page 142
Another Night Thought	142
Beer Posture	143
Below Bungalow	143
Bifurcated – Half Truncated	144
Blessing Of Art Craft	144
Brain Slivers	145
Circular Frustration	145
Conceived	145
Environment	146
Exclamation Sideways	146
Expert Docking In Newcastle	147
Friend Relations	151
Heat	151
I Dream Of Life	151
Ideas In Trees	152
In A German Forest	153
In Group Dressing Room	154
Initiation	154
Knock Down – Stand Up	156
Litter Dropping	156
Living Too Close	157
Machines	157
March Of Time	157
Molecular Structure	158
On Emerging From A Walk-Way Tunnel To Wait For Tube Train	158
Our Dance	159
Opening For Closing	160
Phone	161
Poster Defacing	161
Railway Sleepers	162
Reply To "Chordless Electric Drill" Newspaper Ad. Sent By Ian Breakwell From Ireland	162
Return	163
Scraped Youth	163
Search Light For Quality	164
Searching	165
Self Note	166
Sharp Saddle	166
Sound	166
Spider's Life	166
The Poy Tree	167
Thought Burn	167
Thought Pressure	169
Too Much For Lunch	169
Two Way Site	170
War On The Ground	170
Water Play	170
Waters Plumbed	170
Whirls Of Brain	171
Xmas Croppers – From Crackers	172
Youthful Optimism	172
Youths	172

noun clown

A

Academia 2009–2010

n. A fungal complaint spread by Platonics that gets under the skin to cause an insatiable itch, principally round the arse.

Academic 1997/10/22

> A PhD, being quite a headful,
> can be simply written Dr.eadful.

Academics & artists 2010

> Academics are those who think that they are preparing for life,
> or worse,
> that they are preparing everyone else for life.
>
> Artists live life.

Acceleration and intensification 1991/02/16

As we approach middle-age, we have got used to the obvious thrills and novelties that excited us when we were younger.

In order to maintain our interest in the many facets of life, we try to accelerate and/or intensify experiences. But these processes tamper with the real speed and correctly-spaced layers of life until we may find ourselves tight balls of condensed matter accelerating out of control.

These results can be experienced inside ourselves as depressions and panics, and outside as technological and electronic explosions which may give us the irreconcilable contrasts of physical comfort, quick thrills, total mental disorder and spiritual vacuum.

If we survive these tensions and can learn from them, we will progress through to old age, handing out advisory phrases like:

"Go steady, boy."

"It'll all come right in the end."

"Slowly as you go."

"Don't panic."

"If you don't do it, some other bugger'll get there and make up for it later."

"Just go out and enjoy yourself."

Advice 1994/09/19

It is better to set a good example than to offer any advice.

Allegiance 2013/09/14

n. A clinging on to the fading hopes of a lifelong friendship.

Analytic 2011/06/22

n. One who is paralyzed between the conscious and subconscious.

Anonymity 1991/05/16

I strive for contented anonymity – and complete uproar.

Anxiety 1992/08/19

n. An insatiable itch found in, or on, most humans.

Apology 2017/09/10

n. A feeble verbal attempt, spoken or written from the conscious mind, to right an irrevocable wrong that was usually commanded into action from the sub-conscious mind. It is therefore useless.

Apples pre 1974 *Fallables p.101*

> Every man to his own straw basket full of apples.
> Usually the ones at the bottom start to rot first,
> but they take a while to discover.

Application 2009

n. A plea made by a very small person who is prescribed an unctuous ointment whose formula has been carefully worked out by a group of very large persons. (apply = to rub in)

Art 1 1987/09/25

> Making art, being creative, is a positive way of using our nerve-ends.

Art 2 1987/10/06

Last evening, I provoked and upset two ladies, ate my mince too fast, slept too fast and woke at 3.30am with the tight fist of indigestion clamped on the tail of an idea which will develop into a major work.

Art 3 1989/09/04

> On creativity: "Believe it and leave it".

Art 4 1990/04/31

Making good art is a healthy way of closing the gap between fantasy and reality. *[refer to Depression 3]*

Art 5 1992/07/09

Usually, more art is exuded backstage than onstage. In most media work, more art is used in the participating individuals' manoeuvring and manipulating during production than ever gets out to the consuming public. *[see also Backstage]*

Art 6 1993/09/29

There is little art in giving members of the public what you think they think they want. There is art in what you've been doing for years; what they think they've just discovered.

Art 7 1994/05/07

The real dilemma of making Art is: is it better to be sick on the public, or sick on your own carpet, and up the walls, just short of your own toilet?

Artist 2009

n. A person who uses subconsciously constructed forms against those who pigeonhole him as 'artist'.

Assessment mid–1970s

> Standing up to be counted is lying down to be numbered.

Avant garde 1 mid–1970s

Those who're "avant garde" have not experienced the ground of the present.

Avant garde 2 late 1960s

> The easiest place to hide is in the "avant garde".

Ron in his studio
1977/02/24

Backstage 1992/07/09

    Most of the best jokes are told backstage, in the dressing room.

Banjo 1988/02/–

    'Banjo' stands for banter and jollity.

Bathwomb 1999/09/19

To bathe, or 'have a bath', is to revisit the womb. To get out of the bath is to be reborn.
   If someone smacks your bottom, it's even better.

BBC fees pre 1974   *Fallables p.84*

Upon complaining to a middle-aged lady at a Hampstead nice intellectual party that the fees from the BBC are ridiculously low:
   "You should be thankful for the privilege of being allowed to broadcast to the British Nation."

Belief 2018/08/27

A common human disorder where a mirage is frantically created and then focussed on in order to avoid the certain knowledge that life is a preparation for death, and certainly not that death is a preparation for life.

Blackbird 2009

n. A plain-looking bird that exists best off the ground to sing the most exquisite and inspiring jazz.

Blame 1991/08/28

    Blame external forces – cover internal failings.

Board 2009

n. A hard surface to sit on, and an even harder surface to sit in front of (and explain things).

Body 1990/06/11

On body-parts: "If you die with anything left, you've not used it right!"

Bother 2010

To paraphrase Confucius,
I am always bothered by someone who says, "No bother!"
[see also: Problem]

Boxes 1975

How open the world is – if one can see out through tin boxes called cars, brick boxes called houses and head boxes called brains.
 Media boxes called televisions neither see out nor see in, but we are constantly peering in to see if they do.

Brain 1 1991/10/23

Man with brain on ceiling got feet in mouth.

Brain 2 1995/11/23

Thinking on one's feet keeps the brain off the floor.

Building pre 1974   *Fallables p.74*

Modern house building gives less room for more people.
When there's less room than that, there'll be no people.

Burn pre 1974   *Fallables p.60*

I bet we burn ourselves out before the Sun!

Business 1970s

Business is business, but it's not art or spiritual enrichment.

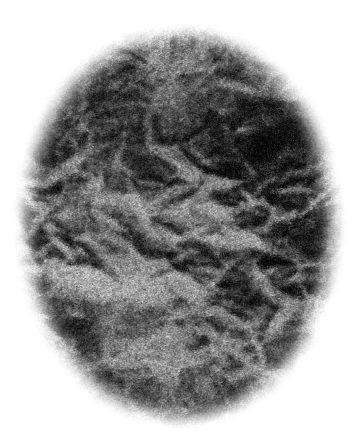

C

C.L.F. 1971, 1993/02/26 & 2012/09/17

The deliberate time-delay built in to any performer's appearance on any stage is called the Calculated Lateness Factor and increases in direct proportion to the real, imagined, or even desired, status of that performer. This also applies to dinner parties and other fantastically imagined important social gatherings.

Care 1992/07/03

When you are advised to, "Take care!" take the least care possible, otherwise you will end up care-worn.

Give care! When you are full of 'care', care-full, give it away by projecting it with great passion into everything you do.

The phrase, "I don't care", has a sulky feel to it and is related to Depression 2. Take 'care' and make free with it.

"Take care!" is, in fact, often said by people who couldn't care less – they have absorbed none and are therefore unable to give any away.

Challenge 1992/08/04

> You challenge others only when you're too tired or weak to challenge yourself.

Clown 1993/12/12

When one finds oneself in the company of fools and bigots, the only options are to play the clown, or leave. Maybe it's also possible to 'leave' mentally – polite but withdrawn.

Collaboration 1993/10/04

> One only ever works with others for a mutual pat on the back.
> If this fails, fulfillment is War.

Comfort 1970s

> Blow your nose on my trousers and I'll put your tears in my pocket.

Communication 1989/09/15

When you don't get a reply to a communication, it's not because the recipient doesn't acknowledge, respect or stand in awe of your thoughts and endeavours, but because of the imagined greater problems than yours that the recipient can't bear to confess.

Composer 1991/05/16

> Composer with too much money, spend it on new woman – easier to play, or structure.

Composers 1988/07/26

> 'Serious' composers are those entirely lacking in humour.

Composition 1990/09/03

In composing music for films and TV, the fee is not for the work done but for the convalescence afterwards.

Confidence pre 1974 *Fallables p.70*

If everyone had no confidence, no one kindly, passionate-feeling human person would ever be approached by any other kindly, passionate-feeling human person.
   Mental Institutions would overflow.

Conflict 1990/10/29

Heat from the abrasion caused by the imagined conflict between your creative ideas and Society's apathy must be projected outwards to warm the earth for new seeds and not held inwards to scorch the soul into bitterness.

Conscious analysis pre 1974   *Fallables p.4*

Conscious analysis of anything is only scorned by me if it's the best you can do!
   There is so much rich super-/sub-conscious flow available from every man that he should learn when to slide the conscious away in its drawer.

Consciousness 1997/07/05

Consciousness is the scum that covers over the Great Liquid Human Chemistry of subconscious activity.

Conspicuousness 1974

A gravy splash on the leg of an airline stewardess shows up more than sick down the front of a drunk.

Control 1 1988/04/07

Eating	is controlled	starvation.
Cooking	is controlled	burning.
Ripening	is controlled	rotting.
Sanity	is controlled	madness.
Swimming	is controlled	drowning.
Living	is controlled	dying.

Control 2 1975

    When I sit in a drab grey room and think of an idea,
        the sun comes out and the room is bright.

Convention 1991/06/04

    Convention is the mother of self-destruction.

Cook book 1989/10/22

    Old cook book with no stains – no use.

Cook life 1990/05/18

I firmly believe that the English tradition of boiling vegetables and pouring the flavour away down the sink is built into our culture to encourage the puritanical Christian belief in enrichment by deprivation! There is another way.

Council 2009

n. A mediocre body that knows best.

Critics pre 1974   *Fallables p.48*

The critics are a funny lot!
They swing from tree to tree.
I don't know where to go from here!
Do they?

Crying 1990/05/31

Crying with laughter balances crying with pain.

Cynicism 2010/08/–

Cynicism merely balances hype.

Ron with tree-root bagpipes and banjo tree, 1972/02/–

D

Depression 1 1987/09/22

One manner of going through life can be envisaged by imagining you are riding on the graph-line of a sine-wave in slow-motion. The inability to swoop smoothly down to know a low feeling, usually camouflaged by a premature shortcut scrambling to the opposite upturn, disturbs the sine-curve balance of life and causes depression.

Depression 2 1989/10/13

> Depression is a sulk in a whirlpool.

Depression 3 1989/10/13

Depression is the temporarily irreconcilable gap between fantasy and reality.

Depression 4 1975

This condition can be brought on by hearing the man in the next toilet-cubicle dropping large aerodynamic bombs when you are struggling to trundle three marbles over the horizon of your purple-strained dawn.

Depression 5 1970s

> 1st Depressive to 2nd:
> "I'll stop what I'm not doing to help you with what you're not doing".

Disgust 1970s

What can be more disgusting than seeing someone doing openly what you do only in private?

Doctor's waiting 1991/04/18

The most pleasant thing about doctors' waiting-rooms is the grumbling sounds of ill-fated breakfasts rippling around as the patients' stomachs articulate feelings their mouths could never express.

Dream pre 197 *Fallables p.46*

I worked extremely hard on this dream! Then, one night, when I was slowly asleep, it issued forth in a rather unexpected fashion and I missed it.

Dribblings pre 1974 *Fallables p.68*

Lots of people talk surface dribblings most of the time simply because they're not teased out from under their brain-covers often enough by other people.

Drugs 1970s

Drugs are often used in vain attempt to see through darkness lightly.

Eccentricity 1990/02/19

There is no motion without eccentricity.

and, years before:

You find me someone admitting to concentricity
and I'll admit to eccentricity.

Elastic bands 1991/06/05

If the Post Office continues to deliver letters wrapped in stout elastic bands at the current rate, we'll be catapaulted into sustained flight by the end of the year.

En-devour 2014/09/24

Our conscious mind seldom recognises the crossover of our activity from joyful enthusiasm to manic compulsion, that condition that devours more energy than is in the tank and continues to acidly eat holes in it.

Energy 1993/06/22

The world only recognises real energy when it's nailed down in its coffin.

Enthusiasm mid–1970s

The difference between enthusiasm and fanaticism is like that of lowering yourself gingerly into a very hot bath, or pouring boiling water over yourself.

[see also Fanaticism]

Equipment 1 1980s

One can write just as important things with a one-inch pencil as with a five-inch one.

Equipment 2 1993/09/28

When you hear someone listing or boasting about the quantity of equipment they possess, it is likely that their talent and passion for life
is inversely proportional.

Fanaticism 1990/05/31

> Fanaticism is enthusiasm minus humour.
> and:
> Enthusiasm is fanaticism plus humour.

Farce 1990/05/18

> The way to damnation is through eternal farce.

Fashion 1 1987/12/10

> The unacceptable face of passion often meets
> the unacceptable pace of fashion.

Fashion 2 1989/09/02

> Ignore the tics of fashion
> for the clicks of passion.

Fashion 3 1990/10/12

> Fashion is the gap between the feet and the floor.

Fear 1991/07/21

> Very often, we only frighten ourselves to enjoy the calm afterwards.

Finish 1976

> One is never finished. One is only ever just starting.

Friend 2013/09/14

n. A close acquaintance who will eventually get close enough to find out your weaknesses and use them for survival.

Friends most of 1993 – took a while to work out

If you review your different individual friends, you will probably find that they represent the contrasting, and often opposing, forces of your character.

Whereas you can maintain a balance, more or less, of your internal forces, when friends' external representations are introduced to one another, there are often extreme clashes over which you have no control.

Future 1988/07/13

> I don't hope for the future, I make it!

God 1992/11/04

When someone exclaims, "My God!" in reaction to a surprising event, it is the subconscious stating, "I am my own centre. I can best deal with/ enjoy/ embrace this event by celebrating, and being in full possession of, my own centre".

God-slogans perceived various dates

> If your problems are deep-seated and long-standing, try kneeling!
>
> Help fight Truth Decay.
>
> If God's your father, phone home today.
>
> Know God – know peace.
> No God – no peace.
>
> Is Heaven your destination? Make sure you're on the Right!
>
> Have you tried contacting God on Faithbook?
>
> (and mine):
>
> Jesus is a lifeless pain – I prefer a painless life.

God Speaks pre 1970 *Fallables p.95*

God speaks, but the stammering is so great that his wig slips off to reveal a fairly well-carved wooden figure.

Golf 1987/09/05

A round of golf is all too often a licence for three-and-a-half-hours of enforced ear-bending.

Good 1997/09/09

There's nothing worse than being good at something.

On stage at the
Bolton Festival,
1979/08/29

H

Hard/Soft 1989/12/19

    People with hard cutting-edges often have soft whetstones.

Help 1993/10/15

    Much of this metaphorically 'helps' the recipient across the road – into the path of an oncoming lorry.

Holidays 1997/09/09

The best holidays are those where you go away to realise that you've got to come back.

Human 1 1992/06/16

A creature that treats animals as humans and humans as animals is odd indeed.

Human 2 1992/08/19

    A human is only an ill-bred animal.

Human Development 1993/08/19

The pattern of human development seems to be derived from the suppression of intuitive thinking by more-consciously 'formula' thinking.

I

Individuality 1996/04/18

Don't be fooled by the gutteral colloquialities tossed about among any group of local workers, or lads out on the piss. You may feel they are intentionally excluding you by their use of this inverted form of oneupmanship. Well, they are using that inverted form, not at you but at each other! This is clear when you notice that each spends more time asking the other to repeat what has been said than actually saying something. They are all stuffing one another. This accentuated garble is an interesting example of the need to be individual, even from within the comparative security of a sheep-pack.
Observed in Glasgow when some workers were leaving a building site.

Infatuation 1990/05/26

A disease, not usually fatal, of deeply-felt short-term pining for a particular person's company when lonely. The loneliness may be in any proportion of physical or mental.

Intention 1993/02/11

When one does not project the full meaning of one's art, expression and passion, but tends towards a watery emission, maybe by panicking towards a cheap short-term commercial application, one is guilty of 'Dilution of Intent'.

When one is given even half an opportunity to explain what one is doing and then reacts in splutters and splashes of all sorts of complicated images, metaphors and new-ideas-in-the-making, one is guilty of 'Acceleration of Intent'.

K

Knowledge 1 1987/09/04

A little knowledge is a dangerous thing. A lot of knowledge is disastrous.
or:
A little knowledge is not as bad as a lot.

Knowledge 2 1990/05/20

To 'know' is really to be healthily uncertain.

Knowledge 3 1991/05/16

One only gains knowledge to use it against others.

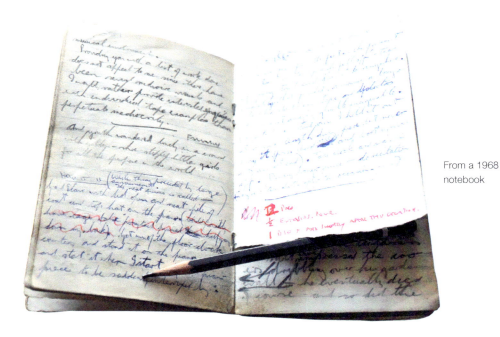

From a 1968 notebook

Late 1991/12/12

> Things are only deemed 'too late' by those who are already set on a panic course.

Law Profession 1989/10/26

The Lawyer's Multi-Storey Block is not his office but a Fraternity Ploy for increasing the dimensions of his office.

Life 1 1990/11/07

> Life is like a game of amateur table-tennis.
> To lose well is to win all, and it's all over before it's begun!

Life 2 1990/09/06

> Life is tough, but if you chew hard and long enough, you get some wonderful flavours.

Life 3 1975

Life is the will to discover and endeavour.
I am not happy when I am not involved in all the possibilities open to me.
Life is experiencing the elements.
Life is passing on life.
Life is not watching others make a mess of it.

Lifelaw date unknown

> The only real law in life is: Do what you can get away with.

Loneliness pre 1974   *Fallables p.98*

If we all realised just how intimately lonely we all are, the word and feeling 'lonely' could be cancelled from life's experience and we would relate to one another in a more true fashion since we would be aware of the limitations of relationships.

Due to our natural resilience and desire to live, discover and perpetuate the species, this common bond would be positive, not negative.

Love pre 1974   *Fallables p.79*

"Daddy, I love you a lot. Please help me up onto your knee so I can pull your hair and punch you in the mouth."

Ron with son Dan, 1971

Machines 1991/02/01

Machines are a human development priority to serve the over-zealous human need for a shortcut to ShangriLa!
 This need actually causes an abandonment of spiritual centre, not a realisation. The only course then is that of constant collision.

Mad pre 1970 *Fallables p.31*

Some people say I'm mad, but I say,
"I'm a great deal more mad than that!"
which brings me back round –
to the front of the extremely sane.

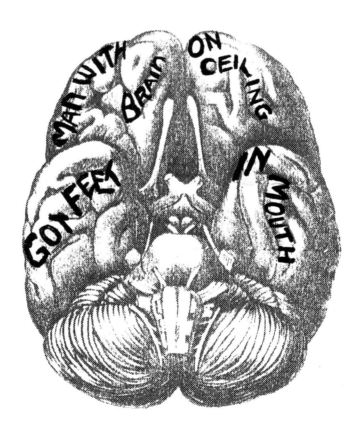

Marks 1969

    Fifty-nine marks on the carpet make a nice bit of visual arrangement –
as long as the manufacturers didn't put them there.

Matter 1975

n. That which is formed into identifiable structures but which produces unidentifiable reactions and inter-reactions.

Media 1992/11/20

The problem with 'The Media' is that it can only really present material to the public in the form it imagines the individual consumer might want to receive it.

    Therefore it has often to adopt a policy in direct opposition to 'the artist' who sets a thing down as he sees it, from inside.

    Of course, since 'The Media' needs the injection of raw ideas from 'the artist' who, in turn, needs to be 'broadcast', compromised deals are struck, but neither party is ever very happy!

    Maybe 'The Media' impresses, while 'the artist' expresses.

Money 1989/10/19

    Money talks! But what a dull and unstimulatory vocabulary!

Movement pre 1974   *Fallables p.54*

    I made a movement! – and everybody looked.

    They made no movement – and I looked.

Needle 1990/11/07

    A stitch in time spares another unwanted pregnancy.

Negro Girls* pre 1974   *Fallables p.70*

    If negro girls didn't wear white coats and white shoes,
you'd bump into them in dark streets!

Nerves 1994/03/26

    A nervous breakdown is a great diagnostic tool for the mind –
if you have the nerve to come through it.

Nervous Exhaustion 1992/07/18

The feeling of nervous exhaustion is like the condition of a chicken that's just had its head cut off. It runs around for a very short time not knowing why it's banging into things.

Newspapers pre 1974   *Fallables p.36*

    The only thing you get from reading newspapers is dirty hands.

    If you must read newspapers, read old ones.
These show up the lies of the society clearer.

Nourishment 1990/03/26

    I like to bite the hand that feeds me – it's more nourishing.

---

* When *Fallables* was released in 1974, this phrase was
in common use and was not considered derogatory.

O.T.T. 1991/05/16

    In these times of MOR, I am going OTT with LP and CD.

Opening for going through pre 1974   *Fallables p.1*

If one is not true to
and fails to realise
one's expressive possibilities,
one is liable to be legally sued by oneself
for misrepresentation.

Openings 1973   *Fallables p.49*

We are all so lonely in our minds that when the slightest opening appears for expression, we pour much more out than need be presented – which soon clogs the opening.

    But we need to pour out as much as possible (arguable) and the recipient wants to hear as little as possible!

[see also: Loneliness/ Outlets/ Platform]

Outlets 1973   *Fallables p.23*

If one doesn't have the outlets, one seldom bothers to manufacture the goods.

[see also: Openings/ Platform]

Outrage 1990

    I never regret being outrageous.

Overload 1997/10/03

    Just because you can do something, doesn't mean you have to.

Pace pre 1974 *Fallables p.45*

A tottering old oily fellow kicked the cafe door open,
after he'd opened it with his scrawny hand.

How out of pace things are with themselves.

Passion 1994/09/25

Passion prevails over technology.

Past mid–1970s

In stepping back too far to admire the past,
you will more than likely stumble and fall heavily over the future.

Penny 1993/10/23

A penny saved is another useful washer
unobtainable at the hardware store.

Perfection 1992/02/15

The only people who don't look funny and misshapen
are models and those in commercials.

Performance 1992/08/08

The first, and best, piece is called 'Tuning Up'.
The next piece is called 'Blame The Environment'.
The last, and worst, piece is called 'The First Piece'.

Performance Aspects pre 1974   *Fallables p.73*

When an audience demonstrates for an encore from the performers, it is supplying its own encore by performing its shouting, clapping, raving, etc., to the performers.
  Does this show a desire to be involved in the performance?
  When one has told a friend about a stage performance or some media utterance that one feels he should go to see, one has performed that work to the friend and partly negated his need to see the work for himself.

Perversity pre 1974   *Fallables p.91*

I have noticed a tendency of (I meant to) do the opposite of what was meant. I just wrote a 'w' for an 'm' and frequently do 'k' for 'g', also 'p' for 'h' and 'f' for 'l'.

Pets 1990/05/03

  Many people keep pets to do to others what they dare not do themselves.

Philosophy 1 1990/08/–

  Real philosophy is the ability to understand someone else's philosophy.

Philosophy 2 1992/11/14

Philosophic conversation is designed to make more problems in the world than there ever were before.

Platform 1973   *Fallables p.23*

When one finds a sympathetic platform for an idea, many more ideas are stimulated which, although having no sympathetic platform, may be strong enough to create their own.

                               [see also: Openings/ Outlet]

Politicians 1994/03/26

  I'll let them get on with their work, if they'll let me get on with mine.

Present–Future 2018/11/–

> I prefer the pleasure of the present to the fate of the future.

Problem 2010

> To paraphrase Confucius (again),
> I always have a problem with someone who says, "No problem!"

Profession 1990/10/28

n. An occupation in which the necessary qualifications are got by the public's paying for one to continually practise on it.

Professional 1991/03/20

n. One who is paid by the public to continually practise on it.

[rearrangement of Profession]

Progress 1976

> Isn't man's progress actually a fulfillment of his weaknesses?

Protection 1975

> In protecting oneself from getting tired, one gets absolutely exhausted.

Proverbs 1975 – 2010

> He who laughs loudest has sadness to match.
>
> A rolling stone squashes insects.
>
> A stitch in time sews up the mouth.
>
> A bird in the hand shites on your palm.

Rabbit 1992/06/15

> Skinning a rabbit is like helping your first girlfriend out of her first bra.
> or,
> helping your grannie out of her last coat.

Rainbow Bit pre 1974   *Fallables p.39*

Just cos there's only a little bit of one side of a rainbow showing is no reason to regard it lightly.
   I don't suppose you'll be able to climb up half of that anyway.

Religion 1987/09/10

> Religion is simply philosophy in (a state of) panic.

Robbery 1989/09/15

> Man in old coat no get robbed.
>
> > Man in old coat no make material progress.
>
> Man in old coat no need to make material progress.
>
> > *[last 2 lines added 1989/10/24]*

Rules (real) 1990/11/07

1. Never wait for anyone, for if he does eventually arrive, he will be one up and you will certainly be one down!

2. Sod 'em all.

3. Do what you can get away with.

4. Share a smile and a cuddle with anyone who's trying too hard at numbers 1–3 above.

S

Science of thought 1980s

Just as man's constant rearrangement of the balance of plants is essential for his physical survival, so his rearrangement of the balance of thoughts is essential for his mental survival.

See Straight 1988/10/–

To see straight, one has to think round corners.

Sensation 1994/09/02

Achieving the sensational is easy.

Observing the quirks in the commonplace is far more interesting.

Shift 1993/10/04

People continually shift carriages in trains in the fruitless search for a better life.

Shoulders (round) 1988/12/23

Many people get round shoulders from too long a dwelling on that most pleasurable moment of lying hunched in the bath in order to let the hot water wriggle into their armpits.

Shyness 1990/09/03

Shyness is healthy uncertainty, until it grows inwards.

[connected to Timidity]

Sick 1978

The bowl was clean, but the top of the cistern was splashed with sick.

Sincerity 1989/10/26

Nowadays, at the back-end, or arsehole, of the 20th Century, 'Yours Sincerely' at the foot of a letter more often means 'Yours Sin Sneer Lie'.

Smoking 1 1992/11/18

        He who smokes is only half-lit.

Smoking 2 1994/09/21

One unforeseen problem arising from the current No Smoking Witchhunt is the sudden unmasking of the clashing blend of old breakfast and cooking stenches effusing from all forms of public gatherings: queues, public transport, banks and post offices.

Solution 1970s

        For every solution, there's always a problem.

Space Notion 1975

In the future, instead of playing with the thought-molecules in our brains (making art), we'll be playing with the molecules of space, other worlds and other forms of matter out there.
   Because computers will get so developed that they can simulate human brains, we'll cease to have the need to look inwards and start looking outwards.

Splashback 1991/08/30

        Only man who wear shorts experience urinal splashback.

        and

        If you take the 'pee' out of 'splash', you get 'slash'.

Standards mid–1970s

        It's not much good working hard at beating the mediocre.

Statement made before knowing how to work properly pre 1970

Fallables p.100

New thoughts come when you need them.

But when you need them, you are out of practice with drawing them forth so, by the time you've got practised, you're on to a new set of thoughts which need a different extraction technique – which has to be practised!

Stillness 1991/04/18

The senseless but amusing contortions displayed by humans in most activities merely show to what extent they are frightened of remaining still.

Stimulation 1980s

There is a faint foggy line between feeding the senses with stimulation and abusing them.

Suicide 1 1991/07/10

This act is often not really to do with taking oneself off to extinguish an unbearable pain.
   The real wish is to go out spectacularly, spitefully leaving behind a performance hard-etched on the minds of the living.

Suicide 2 1993/01/14

It is better not to commit suicide on a dull day because the next day may be bright.

Suicide 3 sometime 1994

        Never commit suicide until the daffodils are out.

Sun pre 1974   *Fallables p.59*

                Don't despair,
              Clouds and Storms
          still have the Sun behind them.

Superiority 1992/07/18

Human superiority over animals seems to rest in the incredible ability to let the subconscious mind commit all sorts of mental and physical atrocities so the conscious mind can stand well back and blame it.

Surprise 1992/12/06

Let all the best things fall out of the cupboard when you've stacked them not to.

T

Talking 1 pre 1974 *Fallables p.85*

    Talking is all right – if accompanied by an adult.

Talking 2 1991/09/13

    Many people are too busy talking to remember what they've said.

Technology 1995/09/11

    Technology expands to fill the nervous system.

Time 1 1990/05/18

    It's just as well that time flies, otherwise we'd all have sore feet!

Time 2 1970s

    There aren't enough days in the hour.

Timidity 1987/09/21

Every person is truly timid. Having the self-confidence to admit it opens the way to an enjoyable life.

Tiredness 1990/10/10

For every tiredness barrier broken in meeting deadlines necessary to accomplish a creative task, one must reverse one's way back through all those barriers in the correct sequence in order to recuperate and be properly ready for the next journey, otherwise tiredness is semi-permanent.

    In the case of non-fulfillment, the tiredness felt is a consequence of being stuck somewhere between barriers, able to proceed neither forwards nor backwards.

Toothbrush 1993/10/13

An old toothbrush is not useless. It gets into crevices that the designer never thought of.

Train Travellers pre 1974   *Fallables p.26*

Why do train travellers and see-ers off always say the most meaningful things to each other just when the train is actually moving off, gathering speed and making them further and further apart?

Travel-theory 1971

When you're on a train and facing the direction of travel, you decide that your future lies ahead of you.

When you're sitting with your back to the direction of travel, you are your future and are in front of your own thoughts.

Tree pre 1974   *Fallables p.64*

A tree that has no leaves in Summer has insect and animal life growing inside it instead.

Two ways – at least pre 1974   *Fallables p.83*

1. Some rampant males go sticking their members into places that were not originally designed for them.

2. Some males, mistaking the original rules of their membership, go crashing with a variety of lies through various-shaped doors to other clubs.

Universe 1970s

My eyelids contain the universe.

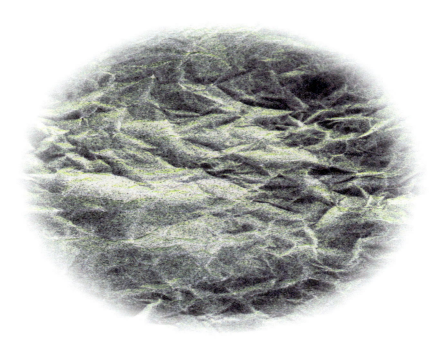

Virus 1990/01/11

Nowadays 'being possessed of the Devil' is to have a virus. The brain chemistry is altered to produce illusion and emotional instability.

Wallpaper 1992/09/20

Many people are avid installers of flowery wallpaper to camouflage and house the insects and other 'creepies' that lurk in their own corners.

War 1991/10/26

Many individuals are so fond of war that, when there isn't a good one on, they make their own.

Wattage 1991

In modern electric music, Wattage should be converted into Twattage.

Waves 1988

Much of the matter of life can be described by waves. The happiest folk are those who can balance the high points with equal knowledge of the lows.

Work-party 1990/05/25

n. A celebration, by any group of workers, sub-contractors or advisers on any job, of the imagined failings of the system and its management.

World Problems 1992/08/19

Could the problems of the World be a direct result of the nuclear mushrooming effect of individuals' need to assimilate all outside anxieties in order to see their own anxieties clearer?

World View 1990/11/07

The world's a bastard! And haven't a lot of people spent a lot of time fruitlessly seeking its parents!

Y

Young and Old 1973

Old ladies who waddle and fuss only look funny to young ladies because they try to be neat and fashionable which merely shows up their ample rumps and over-confined wobbly breasts.

Young ladies who strut and pout only look funny to the older ones because they are so confident and fashionable in their imminently obsolescent attire as to conceal their real unawareness of the slow mangle of life's washing, wringing them out and thinning their fibres.

The old ladies are so busy fussing and wobbling that they cannot pass on their energy – it appears only as beads of sweat on their noses.

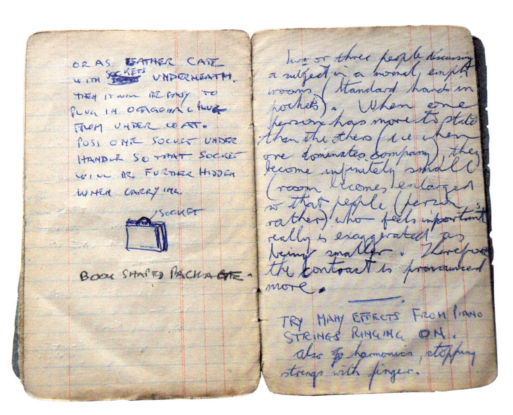

From a 1965 notebook

Reading further

Bierce, Ambrose: 'Enlarged Devil's Dictionary'

Chuang Tse (Zhuang Zhou) – Taoist writings (4th–3rd Century BC)

Flaubert: 'Dictionary of Accepted/Received Ideas'

Goethe: 'Maxims and Reflections'

Lao Tse (Laozi) – Taoist writings (6th or 4th Century BC)

Lin Yutang's works – 'The Importance Of Living' first, then practical philosophy, translations, biographies, novels

Potter, Stephen: everything

Rochfoucauld, François de la: 'Maxims and Moral Reflections' (or equiv.)

Various dictionaries of quotations

stage rage

A Bit Of Paper 1971/2

A bit of paper!

Where's your bit of paper with your life-instructions on it? Be sure to get one when you leave. Maybe one will come in the post tomorrow, or the next day. Then you can buy a sticky bit of paper and send the unsticky one to wherever it tells you. And what of all the discarded ones lying about the streets? People throwing their paper-works-life-works away.

Paper dart of a ten pound note.
Paper fart of a pulp-stuffed throat

(caused by eating paper, you know).

A Great Deal Of Mouth 1966   *[normal speech]*

I'm chuckling all the way up the tube train line,
but one old woman's got white shoes (dented),
and lipstick halfway up her nose –
which makes a great deal of mouth,
but little to say on it.
And, has your plastic handbag fallen apart yet?

On stage at the Third Eye Centre, Glasgow, 1979/09/01

A Pleasant Scene 1969

A large black-winged bird was about to fly out of the grass stems when the Sun flocked through the misty atmosphere. Certainly, a stillness was about, and pastel colours were all subtly apparent.

A few miles away, another world exploded and the remnants and bits of smoke descended on the bird and made it cough eight times. Some grass stems complained but were placated by the bird's exclaiming that at least the weekend gardeners would not now get the chance to poke and prod about their roots.

The grass stems were pleased and waved about to get some benefit from the Sun's filtered flocking.

Before too long at all, thirteen chimneys, and four more, marched in and delivered such acridity that this pleasant scene was temporarily not to be seen (not even by stretching the imagination). And the solitary lady kneeling in the naked brown window of a house that flashed past just couldn't make out what life was all about, so she stayed there for ever (according to stop press reports in all the national newspapers).

This little interlude had given the sun just enough time to change the scenery to a delightful orangy-red and little wisps of cloud-formations curved round it in admiration and pleasant waves of good feeling. The bird flew languidly misty to savour this thing which hadn't occurred for three-and-a-half weeks, took off his black suit and gave it to a large worm who was about the place. The worm ate it immediately for best value and the sun approved by intensifying its wispy atmosphere to a purply-orange. The solitary lady made an ecstatic attempt to leap through her own life, but the glazier had used a very thick one to prevent little boys throwing their soft spoons and drinking cups through it.

This scenario used up so much of the Sun's energy that it had to retire for the evening, followed adoringly by wispy mists and clouds, all showing their gratitude for a lovely eighty-three minutes of natural essence.

A Useful Brick pre 1970   *Fallables p.28*

A little Brick stood up one day
and said, "I'll build a house!"

He found a mate and Fuck Fuck Fuck
but dear oh dear they had no luck
until a lorry smeared in muck
did come along and up did pluck
their red-embarrassed toil-baked selves
and took to man who digs and delves
who needed them to make a womb
for giving compost rotting room,
and after years of frost and rains
the Brick was split and coursed with veins,
and bugs that help compost to loam
came wending through and set up home.

So Brick, who had at first dismay,
now had no room to grouse.

Abuse 1970s

> In England, it's called 'shit'.
> In Scotland, it's called 'shite'.
> In Wales, it's called 'England'.

Add Minister 1971/05/14

"Don't worry," said the minister of the clergy of the church, "with this white collar of neck and soul support, I'll calm even the sweaty-knickered fat ladies at jumble sales". Which he did – by taking off his collar, being careful not to show his underarm condition, and whipping them in a frenzy of enlightened orgasm. Their flowery-patterned rumps giggled up and down as they bounced about trying to fit $7^{5}/_{8}$ size hats on $49¾$ size rumps.

    The minister beat the cherries on the hats into jam which was then promptly bottled and advertised by a scrawny-necked, 'Oh Haw Haw' lady who hadn't quite got her shaving technique together. The minister's wife was mildly on heat in the kitchen as the tea-stained tea-towels parted to reveal a man with a bulge – and that wasn't his beery gut, either. "Ah! Ha! Look who's here!" he said. "Just in time for a cup of leaves of tea. Can I pour you one? That's a nice dress – it's not often we get the opportunity to see your nice leg muscles." Whereupon, she heaved up her long-sought-after dress and, poised like a farmer's wife about to lay an egg, ripped off a quick leg muscle, tweaked it round his neck and jammed a pair of extremely well-confined breasts over his bulge with such impact that tea-steam spurted afresh from the urn and the tea towels fell down in suggestive patterns on the stone floor, itself returning to a lava-like form and flowing out under the door to do over a few sheep.

God was nowhere to be found, and only a few relics and bits and pieces could be detected dongling from the underside of the odd sheep.

A bicycle rode up and fell over. Three minutes later, the policeman of the area puffed into view. Failing to get his policeman's helmet off in time, he missed the extra-sensual delight of the vicarage door-knocker and steamed straight into the act of licking his well-propelled pencil and poking out a sheep's eye. He quickly ripped off one of his coat buttons and filled in the cavity, muttering something about "seeing in a more lawful way" and bounded off on his hooves of leather to locate the man who began this tale.

The minister was soon spotted – trying on a very fine lady's bicycle which he was thoroughly testing by riding all over his wife and her new-found tea-mate, collectively sinking slowly into the lava – the minister making sure he got nice tyre marks and his initials imprinted on it. The policemen gasped and blew his whistle seven feet into the plaster of the ceiling.

"It's too late, of course!" shouted the minister. "It's the Great Treacly Flood. It's happened – I knew it would. have you heard the one about the Irishman and the Scotsman in the bog in Heaven?"

But the policeman had spotted the minister's wife's grey knickers and, like all sensible gentlemen, was trying to see if more could be "casually noticed".

"I've cu-!!" the man with the enlightened bulge was about to say, but disappeared for at least a very long time – with bicycle tyre marks all down his back.

The minister threw his 1931 lady's model at the door and dived out into a sheep, shouting that he'd "found God" – well, maybe a few relics and bits and pieces anyway. The policeman picked up the fossilised minister's-wife-and-man off the mattress, put it onto the old armchair through which a rigid minister protruded, trundled everything into the corner, put his boots back on, switched off the Great Verevision Box and went tromping off into the gloom that is known as 'all the things in life that man has craved for'.

Ailments 1970s

"D'you know, I've got *another* cold coming."
"Couldn't bend down this morning – it's my back."
"How *am* I going to manage with this elbow?"
"Then I went and cut the *other* finger!"
"Went right over on this ankle – came up like a football."
"I couldn't *see* for the pain."
"Whenever I get that ache in the back of my head, I feel like I'm going to die."
"Dropped my glasses, went to pick them up, cut three fingers on the broken lens, stood in the cat's dinner, banged my head on the cupboard door *and* messed up the table cloth with all the blood."
"Sixteen stitches and *then* knocked it on the corner of the wall."
"I can't stand up for fear of falling down."
"When I get those dizzy spells, I just pack up and go to bed."
"I've been back to that hospital four times and *still* they can't find anything wrong."
"It's that twinge when I half turn."
"It's only one toe on each foot that's dead."
"Had to give up everything 'cos of my ankles."
"You want to see a *real* bruise?"
"That's nothing – you should have heard the noise when I had all my teeth out."
"It's only a slight ache in the eye."
"I'm all right as long as I keep moving."
"If you stay in, she gets at you, an' if you go out, you get run over."

On stage at the Third Eye Centre, Glasgow, 1979/09/01

Alphabite 1972

[First half: loudly exclaimed with arms outstretched. Second half: stage whisper]

Ah, free to B and C, and F and P!

Appearances 1978/05/19

"What shall I wear with my new blue suit?"

"My neck doesn't come out of the collar well."

"If I sit slightly forward, my hair won't hang over my fresh white collar."

"My scarf's got the name tag hanging down so my light-brown hair will have to be curled up slightly to show it well."

"My suit doesn't suit but I'll sit up straight."

"That lass with the frizzy straw-coloured hair and the peach cardigan – they don't match."

And ties
that match eyes,
and browns
for frowns.
(Old ladies – maroon.)
Pulling trouser-legs
to ease the knees –
release-at-the-crease.

"We are not nodders. We don't shake our feelings all over our lapels."

"My parting creeps lower –
to release more –
to cover less."

Barbed Wire 1971

Loopy Loopy barbed wire,
wonder who's inside.
Windows full of metal bars.
What *is* there to hide?

"All sorts of mal-formed things,"
so the System says.

(Imagine two suited and hatted individuals breaking their lives scrambling over an old partially-dead twisted oak tree to envelop it in barbed wire.)

And over the hill came a deputation from the Official System and as it got to be quite near it opened its mouth to give ruled judgement. But the barbed wire that was its teeth ripped its own lips to bits.

Bitter Letters pre 1974   *Fallables p.6*

Dear Aura of Life,
Thank you for jumping
and kicking me in tender places
cos it gives me something to cuddle –
a bruised gut.

                                                 Dear Internal Thought,
                      Thank you for the consoling sympathy
                             about my swollen flesh –
                            it makes me strong again
                   to admit Life's Aura into my world.

Bloomers pre 1974   *Fallables p.47*

Nice old lady, no matter how often you tug at your woolly skirt hem to persuade it to cover your knees, I can still see your new shining cream bloomers!

Brass Butterfly 1969

And people to'd and fro'd, and one woman had actually pinned, just out of range of her left tit, a brass butterfly with a glass-glittered body that was so fat that any kind of flight would have been quite impossible. The wings all had fearful cancerous growths bulging from them. Sandwiches were consumed with, at best, two fingers, a thumb and a closed-aperture mouth.

    Britain sagged on with her tits drooping at night-time and reasonably tethered with string and other coarse filaments in the daytime. There was such discrimination between the transition stages of night and day that conversation, with a closed-aperture mouth, caused people to be distracted and to lose Life which, escaping through the ears, had already made abundant shit on the tops of their personalities. Wigs and hats became necessary to keep the shit at bay and, in the twinkling of a brass butterfly, people were clad in layers a great deal more complicated than skin, and feelings through all this stuff became very difficult.

    Fashion was soon created so that other people making these humane coverings could standardise production and make more gangrene notes – to buy rather special coverings for their own problems. Some of these special people afforded a great deal more than glass and metal butterflies and, by whipping Fashion into further frenzy, were soon barging around in large vehicles, absolutely necessary for carrying all their stuff. There was so much checking necessary to see that all the decorations were in the correct order and place that collisions became very frequent.

A wide variety of bearded and shaved gods were soon to be seen sitting on clouds and other convenient transitory substances so that these collisions could be averted by everyone steering in the same direction. In fact, it soon became law that steering wheels were to be locked in place for minimum deviation from the way towards the chosen god. Of course, you've noticed, since the gods couldn't all sit in the same place in the sky, people collided twice as much, having set their sights on their particular god (those who had straying eyeballs were issued with Regulation Blinkers), and the most dreadful fights broke out at collision points, because no-one could see the other person's line of travel. Travel soon became impossible and people simply stayed at home, waving innanely at their gods from behind the glass of their windows. They had to stay in that position too, since all their body-decorations totally filled the rest of the room space. Well, as you can see........

British Wail 1970s   *[Adjust prices to suit current exploitation.]*

British Rail Coffee – 13p

This may be fresh real coffee, or old, boiled grey, formerly fresh real coffee, or instant coffee. It may be served with fresh milk, or powdered milk, or sterilised, paralysed milk. I make that nine possible varieties of 'white' coffee. That does not include strengths of brew, which vary widely, wildly.

Over the past two years, instant coffee has become predominant, for the tumbling of a spoonful of powder into a paper cup at less than 1p a shot must appeal to the dispensers. When this is served 'at your seat, Sir', the silver-plated pot which used to contain a real fresh brew from actual ground coffee beans now issues forth plain water, approximately boiling and splashing down in weak attempt to excite the 'soluble solids of real coffee' which have already been fairly shagged out through processes of alternate steaming and freezing in the curly tubes of technological man's twitching to improve our living standard. If we want 'white' coffee, British Rail serves us a tiny plastic potty off another silver-plated article. Prising off the potty's sealed top is not so easy if the carriage lurches, which it frequently does, for then we have premature ejaculation – from man and material – and even if we do get the stuff into the the foul-smelling liquid, there is only a slight change of colour to dark-brown. It is very unusual to get another little potty either, because the dispenser has long gone up the train to make his fortune.

British Rail advertises in its own carriages to encourage passengers not to drop litter. While travelling from Euston to Birmingham recently, I watched a ticket inspector punch a little piece of confetti-like litter from everyone's ticket, adorning floor and seat. Maybe this was the organisation's subtle psychology of suggesting to its customers that they were in fact wedded to British Rail.

As he waddled on through his duty he also decorated the comfortable, stream-lined, double-glazed, air-conditioned interior with the largest stomach, pushing out in front of it the dirtiest waistcoat I have ever been amused with.

The gold-frayed braid on his cuffs disappeared in places into an over-covering of old dinners and other matters. His jacket, in which the aspect of pockets had long worn away, was one big receptacle with two side-slits which had been previously enlarged and badly sewn up again. This motley shining litter-bin must have contained several issues of the complete ticket-collector's manual which had never been fetched again from the depths, and as this modified man-machine coaxed his fat-covering on its pulsing, swishing journey, it reminded me of a pack of unruly hounds leaping and snapping in all directions at people who, protecting their good frames, were so distracted as to forget that the human managing this ensemble was not aware of anything save getting up and down the train and back to spill more tea and bits down his wasted coat.

The resilient suffering human passenger race survives – to continue.

Conservation Piece pre 1974 *Fallables p.75*

"Sycamore! Sycamore!"

"I can't," said the Sycamore, "I'm sick enough already!"

Cubicle 1967

As I was seated in a cubicle in the bog, a fellow came in for a pee, and talked softly to himself.

During his excretion, he coughed awhile and spat two amazing things which slid gracefully down the porcelain.

Dance pre 1974 *Fallables p.80*

> Dance when rhythm hits.
> Nod head politely – won't do.
> Gyrate, leap, ankle, exercise.
> Gut throb ear dance.
> Foot and leg trot.
> Neck wrench – thought tornado.
> Whaaaaaaaaa!

Dinner Party 1971 *Fallables p.43*

Clog up the world with art!

Which way round is Life?

Are people in cities topside up?
Are humans in meadows?

Whose thought are you?

"I'll swop you four sentences on 'Which House You'd Prefer To Live In' for three on 'When I'm Depressed'".

 So the interested parties projected barbed missiles at each other from behind their quick-to-assemble, remains-upright-in-a-force-9-mixed-metaphor barricades.
 When, after 3 hours, melon with glace cherry and the wrong spoon, casserole chicken, 4 bottles of cold red wine, fresh fruit salad with soapy tinned cream and far-too-strong instant coffee, it was realised that their missiles, although of different manufacture, were terribly equally matched, they all suddenly had to go home.

Dog-Walk 1966

[First half: loudly exclaimed with arms outstretched. Second half: stage whisper]

Five dogs went for a walk –
and there was a man on the end!
But the man's shoes was all worn out –
and the dogs won't pay for the re-soles.

Drugs 1971/2

"I can fly!" he shouted as he swam down the hypodermic needle shaft, only to catch the seat of his seat on the point of the point as he was half flushed, half scrambling through the hole at the end.

He found himself:

> (a) sitting on an absorbent velvet-like stuff which dried him off and cracked his shell beyond repair;
> (b) being spasmodically pumped up a tunnel in which little green men came out of the murky pinkness and limpetised themselves to him, tearing bits off his suit and binding him rigid with purple rope.

Finding himself in either of these situations, he concluded.

Enthusiasm 1971

I feel a leaping in my chest.

It's not my lunch.

Failure pre 1974   *Fallables p.42*

"I admit failure!" he wrung from his sodden brain.

> "You give up too easily!" loudly twitched his panicking employer.

Half a breath dimly lit itself exactly in the middle of his head. When the browny-purple dust had blown away, the deserted concrete expanse was ready for more litter-clutter.

On stage
at the Third
Eye Centre,
Glasgow,
1979/09/01

Fear The Lord 1980s

Fear the Lord
for he is of your own baking –
in a sky of leather
with a golden crust
and a soft nutty centre.

Fear the Lord
for he is of your own baking
in a sky of leather,
emitting ominous clouds
of too high an oven.

Give early 1960s   *[loud whisper]*

Give me some thoughts from your heart or brain
'cos people say it's all the same.

But you're meant to love me from the brain
which people say is all the same
as the heart,
which films in the 1920s
prove to me, and you, and Jane
whom you love now.

Give – Give – Give me some thoughts
for the insane heart of my brain.

*[Words for the first multi-track tape piece I ever did.
The accompaniment was made
by using a jug-blowing technique
with a cardboard tube, overlaid.]*

Glasgow – an aspect pre 1974   *Fallables p.81*

An extremely fat and gummy bus conductress wobbles and frets and poddles and wets on the opposite seat to me of the bus's lower, non-smokers' deck in fierce counterpoint to the holey road beneath. Grey-white chewing gum matter presents itself spasmodically at her mean Glasgow lips, alternating with her cigarette which is sucked when it is not rolling druggedly about on top of her ticket-issuing machine or charging up and down, and off, the long seat, dropping its fire and ash amongst the plastic cups and other less white rubbish, further propelled by chewed and muttered whinings about the discordant duet of erratic driving bus man and undone Corporation road holes.

   A scrawny cloth cap and neck nods to the Pope who has got himself several small stalls supported with bent cardboard boxes scattered variously along the roadsides. Many various-sized painted plaster images are on sale and quite a number with large pieces broken off are being brought back in torn imitation plastic leather bags, only to have it explained that the purchasers probably have not been confessing enough and absolution is only granted by their completing a 13-page questionnaire through which they get a special adhesive that breaks all mends.

   Three 14½-year-olds are glimpsed taking turns with an 11 inch breadknife at stabbing a derelict brick wall. It is surmised that he whose hand slips on the handle of the knife upon impact with the wall has lost – his hand!

   Oh, the blancmange of a conductress bites and wrenches pieces of nail from her fingertips and is well schooled in this art, making them like embryonic heads of pre-life. A crumbly chunk of derelict stone topples off somewhere or other into the roadway, stopping the bus and not before time either, cos it allows a man to rattle down the stairs and nearly reach the gutter before a partly digested steak pie and beery gravy is offered to the land from whence it originated. But there are no workmen available to dig and pick the necessary hole through the bus platform, tar mac, gas pipes and hard core to allow this ecological flow so the matter rests – on the bus platform – and keep fit classes are hastily arranged with coughed shouts from Madam Sweaty Pie to enable the older of the canned bus company to leap this obstruction whenever they wish to dismount. Dogs, of course, have done their street work and further matters have yet to be overcome!

The bus terminus is finally reached and I choose to exit through a 4 inch square window and slide down the caked mud of the tin side, my coat brushing sufficient mud off one area that reveals an emblem which asks me to 'Let Glasgow Flourish'!

God pre 1970   *Fallables p.57*

If God's up there, we're his excrement.

On stage at the Third Eye Centre, Glasgow, 1979/09/01

Grand Search 1966

> "A leuve ya, baby!"

Who is this fellow loving all the time – his wife, perhaps?

Then, he:

> "don't leuve no gal at all".

He'll find her one day – after he's stopped singing all this "leuving" and the gitr strings have stopped ringing. It's all very embarrassing – for me.

Now he's:

> "down in the mines, dark as a dungeon".

Is this fellow dark as a dungeon, or is it the mines?

Anyway, all this time, this fellow is searching, not for his "leuve", or the coal, but for himself – and perhaps he's going about it the wrong way.

On stage at the Bolton Festival, 1979/08/29

Head Boil pre 1974 *Fallables p.7*

Roaring at the ears, shoes melting, wrists wrenchy, teeth and jaw moved big and heavy by 85 steaming black slaves, each with a large wooden handle-bit between his teeth and 3 ropes to manipulate, one for each hand and one clasped in both feet, his waist tied down with leather to prevent any unnecessary movement of bum on bench.

Thus did I emerge from the night tunnel of restless body movement. What hair that is left on my head became steam that wisped past my left eye, a ball that has bounced in and out of many a brain cover.

"Surely I am not alone!" I screamed in a low unreadable voice and, on its return, the echo got grated and serrated through and over multifarious jagged pots that people have built and called 'chimneys'.

"Surrrlllyee-noloan!" might have been the echo's echo but an extremely-dirty-white-coloured Con-dis-corde melted through the flesh of my left ear lobe on its path to a tasty dish of stewed pound notes, and some of the cooks had chartered it to make sure it got there so I didn't receive the echo's echo.

But the serrated gratings must have sufficiently broken the crust of the brick-broken mutilated plastimetal that covers a great deal of the world that is an eyeball, and little light yellow-green stubs poked through, cos the Sun was still up there, way up there, even though someone had devised a new kind of force of matter transference and was attempting to move the Sun to his own laboratory-country where it would be used to grow humlants – in which the old human brain was to be stretched in durable fibrosity and connected inextricably to root and flower, making rings of energy that took their partners for a whaltz or a flexitrot and multiplied their species by being fried on a plasetal plate whose temperature was so great that they never actually touched it but skimmed over, coming off the other side as more-than-when-they-started.

Notwithstandingfor that this is predictably possible, the little light yellow-green bumpouses poked their little selves up (or out, whichever scale you are looking at the plane terrain of the global strain with for) and waved to one another as a positive signal.

And on the third day, some men who thought this to be a favourable sign went forth to water the bumpouses and to bring them to their maturity and wholesomeness.

But they should have used ethylene glycol and not water since the bumpouses were a very very new phenomenon and the little bumpouses melted and formed an impenetrable crust in that area which, from that time forth, served to remind the silly, pea-brained man species that new thinking is needed for new times.

Head-Knock 1966   *[like circus ringmaster]*

Knock on your head and open,
and take your shoes off too,
for "Everybody's happy!"
Hè – Hè – Hè – Hè! – Mooo!!

Heart 1973

"There's my heart! There, through those wintery lacework trees!"

It smiles itself into constantly-changing shapes.

Sometimes it's poked from inside with dry twigs to appear as a jester's hat. Sometimes the wind blows all the form out of it and it swings hooked on one of the trees like a burst balloon.

Holes 1971/2

Men get trapped in holes of their own digging. But, mind you, and you, so many people in high important echoey places tell, no, advise them with menaces that holes are the things to be living in and, since a human is not a human without another human, communication must be effected so, what with the skinned knees and grazed noses got by clambering out of one's own hole to get to someone else's and the broken whatevers got by falling into other and various holes on the way and, to bottom it all, a well-lascerated bum occasioned by the sliding down into that someone else's hole, few people now are bothering to set out at all but sit there in the damp earth with fag-ends sticking to their elbows, shouting at their nearest and costliest with their eyebrows clogged and laden with sticky earth and the odd stone bouncing off and attempting to chip their marble-crusted heads.

On stage at the Bolton Festival, 1979/08/29

Jazz Band late 1960s

All I can write's in rhythm,
'cause a trad band plays,
rhythm, rhythm, hot, hot,
not
really for humans.
It's for a robot, hot, hot;
constant, no build-up.
No sky, no air, just hot
rhythm – and on and on and on —

Sure as clockwork
make the tune work.
People stomp in time.
Where is their stomp going?
Down the drain of Britain.
But their flood of rhythm is but a wee trickle
so the drain won't overflow.

Rhythm is very effective – if built up.

Chonk-a-chonk-a-chonk chonk chonk plong tsh!
Get off yer bum, Mrs.!

The drummer has a terrible ailment.
He is paralysed all but his hands.
Who sat him at his drum set?
Who set his drum?
Who puts the smouldering cigarette in his mouth?
His hand?
Who gave him the rhythm to move his hands?
The leader!
(He stomps his foot as a slight consideration.)

Who gave the people money to come and hear and see this walking, thrashing, expression-lit splodgy mess from the bog of Britain?

Jesus pre 1974 *Fallables p.56*

'JESUS IS ALIVE TODAY! –

if you can call being nailed up, taken down, preserved (mostly with artificial colouring), cheeks rounded out with cotton wool padding, bent into position, propped up, light bulb concealed neatly protruding slightly out of the back of his head for aura effect, wired to a battery strapped behind his back and mouth wired for peaceful benign smile, life.

Well, it *is* life – but not very live.

Look pre 1970 *Fallables p.32*

Look here
        and there
                and everywhere
                        for the remains of what might have been.

                                But where indeed?
                Down the lavatory?
Very possibly, even.

Lost And Found late 1960s

"I'm lost!" I shouted over the top of a light dirty-blue car, trying to attract the attention of three red-flushed broken noses belonging to two-and-a-half men whose jackets hung a-swinging like drunken weather cocks and whose heels could be heard a-scluffing above the noise of everything else – yes, but everything!
    I thought I'd do the human thing and grasp them by physical touch, as they do to each other when they're falling out of pubs at night, and Sunday lunchtimes, confessing each to the other that they're inseparable, and rallying up against their assorted misshapen wives.
    Well, at least four motor drivers splintered teeth in many fine jaw clenches as I made to cross Mr. Tar Macadam's clotted arterial throughway. The two-and-a-half men were overjoyed to see the scots accent which I wore as a free pass badge into their lives and vigorously clumped me on the back, irretrievably committing me to splutter the final, "They're open!"

Material Miss pre 1974   *Fallables p.55*

The Trade Winds blew deficits and the workers got so bored striking at every available Sunny Day that they began working really really and blew the gaskets of many a Director's heart. Not that the Directors' Wives were at all troubled by that since now they could get those extra carpets for ceilings and special dog-teeth-mountable tin openers so their little doggy babies could open their own bloody tins of meat.

WHY HAVE PREGNANCY
WHEN YOU CAN HAVE SENSATIONS FROM YOUR POODLE DOG!

Nerves 1978/05/19

A bogey-man touched me on the shoulder –
I turned round –
to the shadow of a thought.

Now – more or less pre 1974   *Fallables p.67*

I glide in bumpy uncertainty through the darkness, my over-positive shoe-step correcting this into the Greater Tomorrow Inclination.

   The city's many chimney pots offer themselves in silhouette against the mildly energised off-black glow, but they neither smoke nor steam while God, lit with 25 watts, claws desperately to glance even faintly out of an over-high stained glass church window ledge.

   Through a cracked squinting window high up in a cracked squatting tenement, a 25 watt woman is wearily flattening her husband's future shirt with a nearly-steaming iron in an environment where the purple sweat and agro *must* eventually print its feeling on the
                            creamy-browny
                         ever so piled up
                      non dish washy
                 ever so squashy
             piled up feelings
         ever so –
      ironed out
    onto the stove
  under the sink
beyond the plug-hole of anyone's conception.

I live on in my own agony.

Reaching out, I can't even burst through the paper bag that envelops my being. I notice a man in a big railway station striding out and pushing a very over-noisy luggage trolley in front of him.

This is the way to proceed in living! – Make such a loud noise in front of you that you drown the thought of your own uncertainty.

Nut 1965

All the world's a nut
that screws on a twisted thread.
All the people in the world go mad,
and take to bed –
weeping and groaning.

Blackbirds in trees and girls with knees
sing love in harmonies,
wearing blackbirds' nests upon their nuts
and falling all over the place in pairs.

On stage at the Third Eye Centre, Glasgow, 1979/09/01

On Going late 1960's

I've got to clear the weeds from my brain
instead of reclining comfortably on a train,
but there's no-one here to pick their nose
or ask me if I'm one of those –
people who might be real.

What do you do when you can't express your feelings
and your friends laugh at you and their girlfriends laugh at you
and passers-by laugh at you?
Do you retreat from the Great Society
and begin a piss-up?
Is reality in the mind a fantasy anyway?
Maybe you're not bothered.

"What the bloody hell's he on about?
He can't even play tunes!"
"Nice arse on that bird!"

Maybe she'll enlighten you, although she's probably been worrying for
the past three days what she smells like and at what stage in the sexual act
she should take off her false eyelashes. I do wonder how long we'll actually
manage to survive the constant barrage of piss-ups, TV and shag-ins.

"What else is left for a good honest liar?"

"A nice cup of tea."

On stage at the
Bolton Festival,
1979/08/29

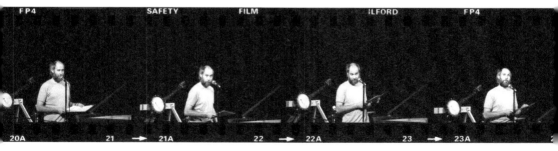

Perception 1976

She snarls at him. He snarls through her.

This rapport mellows through the years until they are both on their backs, lying side by side on the marble slab, smiling at infinity. If you stand back far enough, their gazes appear to fix on the same distant point.

Performance – Bracknell, 25th May 1979

A man sitting at a table near the stage threw a jelly-baby at me every ten minutes or so. At first, I didn't know what they were, being used to people throwing bits of paper and, occasionally, coins. Anyway, I was preoccupied with projecting my best utterances.

When one of the jelly-babies hit me in the balls, I picked it up and, with a loud curse, projected it at his table. To my surprise and joy, it fetched a neat bite out of his empty beer glass right into his lap. There were no more jelly-babies forthcoming!

Afterwards, he explained that he judged how good a performer was by seeing how and when he retaliated.

I got high marks.

On stage at the Bolton Festival, 1979/08/29

Pretty Little Faces late 1960s

Silhouetted houses, brown against the sky
frowning down on humans who might dare to pass by.
Pretty little faces, undisturbed as yet
smile very sweetly – soon they'll forget
what it's like to feel all warm inside
'cos the houses have engulfed them!

But all they've got to worry 'bout
is the colour of the walls
in the nasty black houses!

And as their brains darken
and their chimneys pour forth soot,
their 20 watt bulbs flicker
as they begin to put
their souls in their fires
and pollute the atmosphere
and here, and here, and here, and here . . . . .

*[Performed, with plucked and beaten grand piano, on my very
first John Peel's 'Nightride' programme, BBC Radio, 1968/07/03.]*

BBC Broadcasting House, 1968/08/29:
Ron; unknown poet; John Peel

Pretty Little Girls late 1960s

Pretty little girls with the flickering eyes – don't blow them out yet. The smoke seems to have coloured your eyebrows black, and the charcoal over-fertilised your eyelashes. Really, the aura round your flickering lights is black in mourning.

"Have another sweetie, mother," said the young doctor man with lines on his face and several twitches.

But still the two nice heavily-shaven little girls bit their nails and worried about their supply of razor-blades and face mourning powders, all the while twiddling with their hair and their nails – and their loin cloths – and trotted off for lunch to spend some more of Daddy's money.

And isn't it all nice?
so
Shave your legs and bite your nails
and pull your tights up 'cos they're baggy at the knees.
And really bite your nails,
echoes of your boyfriend's wails.
In fact, bite him too,
it'll do him good.
(I wonder if you should.
Yes.)

On stage at the Third Eye Centre, Glasgow, 1979/09/01

Rise Up Sebastian! late 1960s

[Performed on the album
'As He Stands' RON28]

<u>Scottish, gutteral</u>   <u>Pompous parson</u>

The noo
a coo
                                             was happy.

The noo,
                                             immediately,
she wus crazy fur a wee daisy
                   which she ate with great relish
                           and lived in the countryside
                              which is the land all over.
Ther wus very few daisies left that night.
         So she slept and chewed and slept and woke
                                  and produced milk.
An' we wus a' happy.

Extasies pour from the feet on the pavement
which dissolved.
Trees sprong – – – – Tweeeeeeeeee!
A minister of the clergy of the church extinguished himself
causing freedom for the sprong tree.
And the earth tasted good.
But the lipstick fell off and was never recognised
because it never was.
And the earth tasted better.
Little boys built a home in the rocks and liked it.
And the earth tasted best.

Rise up Sebastian!
till your head meets the clouds
and your feet are emplanted on the blue-grey distance.
There you are viewed by Geraldine Public
who will be quick
to pick
holes in your frame.
Comb your hair quick for you are on view.
Cover your bald bit, polish your nose,
sweep the grey cloud from out of your eye

and the pond from the other.
Geraldine grows impatient –
be quick Sebastian! —
An aeroplane has flown up his nose and he has sneezed and I am dazzled
and the Sun has won.

On stage at the Bolton Festival, 1979/08/29

Round And Round 1967

Round and round we go in our heads
and when that gets too much, we take to our beds.
Who's going to arbitrate?
Yes, who's going to arbitrate?
For everyone's right in their heads.
Everyone's right in their beds.
So, please let me out of my box
cos a lot of people's got locks
on their noses and specially eyes,
on their noses and specially eyes.
And their ears fell off years ago
with too much rubbing the pillow
that's round and round our heads
and specially the ears in our beds
of life and especially life,
of life and especially life –
and 20 watt lightbulbs don't really light.

But then newspapers that get stuffed under chairs can't be read anyway. And that must be the reason that ladies get lipstick halfway up their noses and can't see to shave their knees.

Round and round we go, indeed
there's a lot of people got a need
for bald heads and beards and hairy knees
and trousers that don't get caught up in bicycle wheels or combine harvesters.

Yes, I think you'd better rock yourself to sleep.

Round and round to the sea – in ships,
and pebbles that slip — My Goodness!

                "Whose Goodness?"

Pebbles and shells have goodness within,
and boxes of sweets, not made of tin,
but good honest cardboard! That's no sin!
Sweets in the sea will perish,
or slip from the mouth in ropes
of saliva and mucous and all that's nice,
but confessing this costs such a price
in the heads of those who care to admit
that Modern Society's made of shit,

so, may all those humans who do not fit
rest well in their slippery, pebbly pit.
And, as McGonegall said:
"If you compromise and let yourself be weak-willed,
the less chance you have of being killed."

School Groups – 8.55am 1975

Two little boys subversively smoking surrounded by three swaggering
bigger boys.

One boy affectionately leaning on another boy's shoulder.

Two girls cuddling a wall while giggling.

One boy nearly getting killed
retrieving a bald, greying tennis ball from the middle of the main road.

One tousled ginger-haired boy
chatting to two long-heeled, long-skirted, well-groomed girls.

One girl laughing with her mates
while poking a large sandwich-wrapping out through the railings onto
the pavement.

One four-piece multi-racial female group
dominated by a very tall, loud, flashing-teethed West Indian.

Seen pre 1974   *Fallables p.5*

A pretty, lithe young housewife is stretching up,
pegging a large yellow sheet to the washing line,
her short fashionable jumper
parting company with the top of her tight cuddling slacks.
The wind
is causing cheeky corners of the sheet
to tickle the soft sides of her tummy.

Will her husband come before she does?

Sentence 1973

The elderly ladies attracted the attention of bypassers to inform them of their Christian Aid collecting venture by shaking their money tins so vigorously that the contents formed into charm bracelets which irrevocably broke the lovely teeth of the well-developed under-developed countries that were told they must bite on them.

Shipping Water pre 1974   *Fallables p.25*

He was shipping water at a furious rate
and could plainly see that he was drowning.

Opening his mouth to cry for help, he – !

Talking Man 1966

"Ah Ha," said the man as he spoke,
"the world is exceedingly wrong!
The price of chips has gone up, you see,
and my wife is exceedingly broke".

                    Think of the world.
                         Revolve.
                Think of your relations
                    with the world.

"It's a lot of – – people", said the man who was dribbling spaghetti down his tie and observing the state of the racing horses and other people discussing the state of the world, which is revolving – still – always.

And still the man who was speaking spoke – about nothing – and my dinner's nearly getting cold because I'm observing all this.

The Night Of Nights 1971

I opened my eyes and spotted the luminous dial on my watch.

From out of the blackness came an even blacker pair of large cartoon-like soles of boot (the size of thirteen-and-a-half good-sized paving slabs). They were getting quite near.

"Is there any hope?" I shouted in my ear – and suddenly they disappeared.

Left to my own freshly nude and sticky body, I observed the hiss of the middle of the night. The house shuddered as a car and a big lorry jumped about on the street, 4 floors below. The baby farted.

"What a time for a time for a thought!" I imagined and, fumbling upwards, I uncovered my medium-steaming armpits (without being afraid of adverts in the tubes) and attempted to detach my specially positioned notepad from its hook, at the same time noticing my feeble arms in silhouette against the posh Pifco bedside lamp, which had come to be switched on, to facilitate matters.

Carefully making sure that there was no fluff, or lint, tightly lodged in navel, I began:

I close my eyes, but it looks light,
the blueness does a-dance,
my brain puts up a stubborn fight
as I do ponder through the night
and ideas do on tiptoes prance.

The baby's farted yet again
from within his painted pen.
That paint was fresh a week ago –
is that why my brain aches so?
Breathing is the only sound
as sleep possesses those around –
Oh no, I do forget the cars
that fart away like baby's arse
and make my life seem quite a farce
as I sit up on pillows neat
and not much sweat about my feet –
that's it! at last! I've caught a thought!

My brain splits open and my feet crack. They're very flat and, at the tender age of 9 were marched around an army playground so that they could pick up handkerchiefs and curl round little brass bars.

"Gooooood, goooooood," said the man in the white coat. Well, he couldn't have known much cos I was a little flerrcroonskenternotter.

It was about that time my head split open again and I hid behind sofa-couches to avoid being kissed by little girls whose knickers had associated with some very dubious soap-powders. No manner of trippy piano playing by the short-sighted village piano teacher, with just the right amount of wrong notes jingle-jangling round her wrists, could coax me from behind the wide-spread bum of Mrs. Sofa-couch (with the faded flowery pattern). Yes, of course I was dragged out by many sticky hands, but not without some of Mrs. Sofa-couch's finest rump stuffing between my teeth. This gave the impression of a large moustache – something every boy of 10 needs to exercise his father's razor on. And so it came to pass that I was shaving heads off pimples and pencilling in my potential side burns/boards/chops – with a 6B.

Then my head split open again – anyone can inspect the various clasps and repair jobs done on it. This time I found myself scratching the back of my neck and taking the head off another pimple. But at least I was standing the way I wanted to and didn't have to comb my hair, which falls out of course – to clog up plugholes.

On stage at the Bolton Festival, 1979/08/29

The Postman Carried A Large Tree pre 1970 *Fallables p.29*

The Postman carried a large tree.

Fourteen housewives of varying degrees of nationality climbed, showing the holes and ladders in the upper parts of their stockings. These leg coverings were. And the Postman nearly was.

Well, they jogged along for some time but, as you might care to imagine, there *had* to come a moment when the legs had reached the top of the tree, everyone could see everything and therefore the game had finished. That is, unless the Postman was called out on urgent strike.

Ah, but the district council had caused letter boxes to be melted down and fashioned into stainless steel tree holders, at a great deal too much extra cost, and these were positioned at every dog-relief point so the housewives could be held in suspension at any point in the area and time. This appealed to them as their grocery listing had been long ticked to exhaustion and their husbands were all unsympathetic pathetics. Not forgetting the cat's dinner. Even at this early break in the morning, several husbands had lost bets and were to be glimpsed shouting at themselves in silence in corners.

And the Postman's spectacle was covered in greenflies from the vigorous activity up the tree: "no, but I says to him" – "Really, all right" – "Well" – "and" – "Oh, you've done it" – Must go down to the" – Taps, got to get some" went the song to the rhythm of empty beer bottles dropping into the side pocket receptacles of tree-holder number 29 on the dustmen's route – and the tip-holding pockets for the dustmen were not full or anything cos the ladies had all forgotten their purses, and the paper, folding, crumpled, torn money had long since fluttered down from their knicker-elastic banks. *That* was why the Postman had so many dogs following him! Oh, one houseywife had no knickers, but had improvised her skirt between her legs for the benefit of the television cameras. Ooooooh, how her leg muscles did ache from holding her skirt in this proper fashion – with blue flowers on it.

It was the wrong time of the year for bees.

Nearly all the –

No!

By this time, the Postman had re-negotiated a fresh pair of trousers, for all that dog-relief had worked wonders with the cloth! Now he was fit to continue the game originally set out in this paper concerned with the sociological conditions in factory estates and the attitude of dogs to someone else's underwear.

The Postman carried a large tree.

The Sound 1974

"Sshhh! – A Sound!!" A black and white chequered, sawn-off, endless, elongated sound.

Here it comes, swooping gently down from mid-frequency range. Its patterned ribbon twists over slightly as it sweeps towards me. Now I can just see how each chequer is fitted to the next. Ah, there are little ripples along the straight edges. Here it comes. I see that the ripples have other different-sized echoes running by their sides. What was a straight line is now many wiggly criss-cross ripples. Sandwiched between the wiggles are thousands of hard, clear, highly-polished chips which serve to reflect and bend the patterns of wiggles into yet more components of what originally looked like a black and white chequered castle wall top. The front passes over. What a complex of seeming simplicity! It's definitely inclining upwards now in its path through the universe of my head.

Here, maybe it wants to join up with its beginning! That would be fine for me.– I could watch it forever and be very excited about the slight changes that are occurring in its reflective twisting. I'll just try to get hold of that far leading end and bend it round over — no, I'll need a long pole — quick, where's that — Oh, sawed a bit off it to make a banjo neck! — It's shorter than my arm — Jump! That's what to do — spring up — no, not so fit as I was (and I never was fit anyway). Aach, it's really out of reach — no, there's the tail flapping gently, probably trying to attract my attention.

"Y-y-y-y-y-ya bastard!"

"Creaking Hinges of Universal Bleedin' Thought!"

That last jump's woken me up. What's the time? Ten past two – I thought I'd slept slower than that – it should be at least half past six.

My head's been blocked with catarrh for three weeks. Still, there must be some kind of space in there, otherwise that sound-ribbon wouldn't have chosen to move. If I lie on one side long enough, all the weight of rubbish slops downwards and I can breathe a bit.

"Ecstasy of Pained Foggy-Eyed Sight!"

Here comes the ribbon again from the other side — have to turn over — breathe through my mouth for a while until the catarrhal porridge completes its slow journey.

The sound-band is swooping faster this time — I'll just watch it to see what happens. Ah, it's more of a U-shape — must be trying to join itself up. Looking at it from this distance, it's a mid-range astral moan that's doggedly trying to lose its beginning and its end. Now I see how it moves. This time I'll catch the front and back to join them together. O-o-o-o-oh, it's a bit hot — hadn't thought of that. Turn over again. I'm getting hot too — can't stop, though. If I don't join it up now, it's going to scorch a path through that catarrh and burn away bits of my precious thought-patterns.

"Crusty Cavities of Semi-Realisation!"

"Empty Echoes of Closed Yesterdays!"

"Rigid New Moulds of Old Potted Endeavour!"

"God Save the Power of Flowery Wallpaper!"

I've woken up again. Must be nearly time to — no, it's only twenty past three. How can any man endure such chasms in Regulation Rest Time? How can a man cut his toenails when he's laid flat out, swishing his hot legs like a Russian dancer under the bed-covers to find cool corners to cool them off? He can put the light on — a-a-a-a-o-oooooo — and sit up.

Who's that scowling, rumpled, putty-nosed person in that mirror? Will he live much longer with eyes like that? No, but now they're open, there's a reasonable chance of a few tolerable weeks yet. Lean out — mustn't let the fellow in the mirror see my bum — drag my trousers across. Nail-clippers: front pocket, right. Look at that big bunch of keys — don't need them cos I'm not at home and if no-one's in when I get back, I'll have lost a family, which would be a lot more difficult to find than those nail-clippers. Got'em. Now, where's those feet — here they come. Well, there's hardly anything to cut! No great hooked, sock-destroying talons. A flea couldn't even use one of the clippings as a springboard into the pool of his dinner. Where's that one gone? I like to make a neat little pile and then put it in a neat little place. Still, nine out of ten's a reasonable score. There are no neat little places in this room so I'll throw them into my case. By the jolted time I get back home, nine little personally-grown uniquenesses will be scattered across, or rather, down, the length of Britain.

Shall we follow the adventures of these bright young springboards? We shall not. I think I've fallen asleep at a quarter to four.

No, just had a pee at five to five and now I really am asleep.

Thought Spot pre 1974   *Fallables p.76*

I've got a spot on the back of my head!
I don't wear shirts so that's all right.

I've got a pad at the side of my bed!
I don't sleep tight so that's all right.
I write all right from night to night,
I smile all gay from day to day
even though my face don't show it
dash it –
blow it –
suck it too.
Not the spot on the back of my head!

    Man all doleful   –   all fall down,
      the muscles in his face   –   causing frown,
        the hustle of the race   –   hair was brown,
          now it's all grey – for   –   fall out, pay for,
            bustle to a place   –   get things down.
              'Where?' – Upon a face!   –   not your gown.
                Get them down!   –   that's no good –
             serves to scramble mental food.
             But it's quite good to be so rude!

            and what's more, brother,
      "Lace tablecloths! And have more food!!"

On stage at the Bolton Festival, 1979/08/29

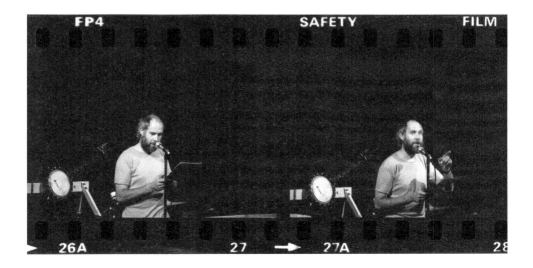

Thought Weave 1971

My thought weaves thick through people's lives. But it appears so thin that it slips through their fingers. How can I make it thinner for me and thicker for them? It gets so thick it clogs my general passage. To where? Oh – out and about – round and through.

"How much money do you get for delivering a thought?"

How much thought do *you* get for delivering money?

"'Ere, you know what the Common Carpet's going to do to my brussel sprouts!"

Ah well, it would seem that most people regard things over too short a ter —

"Bloody big lorries coming through our village!"

Yes, it certainly ties up with wha —

"I'm just not having a daughter of mine going over there to work for them berret-basking Basques!"

On stage at the Third Eye Centre, Glasgow, 1979/09/01

To Be Again Forthcoming With The Second And Third The Next 1970

[Written in three parts (one in each delivery) as some kind of light relief while composing all the original music for John Schlesinger's film 'Sunday Bloody Sunday' – Mozart composed the rest.]

1. The cat sat on the elephant,
who sat upon — "Whose roof?"
The horse went 'baa' to clear his knee.
Instead, he cleared his hoof
which fell off down the drain of life –
indeed, there is a story rife
his head lodged in the grille of life.
(He did experience the pain of life
while searching for his unstuck hoof.)
So, is it not that this is proof
we all should sit upon that roof?
"Whose roof? Whose roof?" It can't be found,
cos we're all anchored on the ground.

2. To stand on the ground
is to spin round and round
with catarrh up your sinus
making thoughts go minus.
So, leap from your shoes
and land on a cloud –
say 'booo' to those blues –
God'll feel proud.
"Who's he?" said the Pope.
"I've tied him with rope.
He's got some hope
cos I'm the Pope!"

Having said all this, the Pope coughed, spun round, and all the catarrh and other thought-rubbish flew from his robe and caused a deal of mess about the world.

3. My God! My God! –
"Whose God? Whose God?"
"The one with the striped pyjamas!"
What's that he's got tucked under his gut?
"It's only a withered banana."

So the Pope, feeling sorry for God, reached round and round his person and found his very own private quintette of bananas and, giving these to God (having first polished them politely on his elbow), he bowed so profusely that God just had to acknowledge – with a fairly animated nod.

The Pope, having unbalanced God to just the right extent, stabbed him all over the cabbage patch with a very erect cucumber.

To The Sterile Village Of Bothwell, Lanarkshire pre 1974   *Fallables p.86*

I've been shut in!

Claustrophoberised!

Everyone looks so brisk in fresh suits of upright postures, so stiff and tense their buds won't open. Any buds that do manage it do so with such energy that they propel themselves away to project their seeds into wilder gardens.
   Many people carry secateurs and prune the heads off other people with flicks of the wrists and cracks of the brains.
   A Great Tightness lies on most pavements unleashing itself round all passing ankles. For those people who can sever their own feet and lurch away, they get it round the neck later from a special breed of Tightness that lives in the baskets of flowers up lamp posts.
   To cap it all, the Devil has taken over the church and sits impaled on the spire with a long snaky whip sorting out anyone who's left.

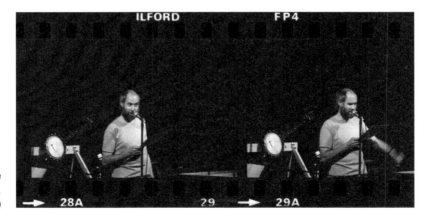

On stage at the Bolton Festival, 1979/08/29

Today 1967 *[Over-acted, as many would do Shakespeare.]*

A fire of smoke!
Is Britain burning?
No, it's the ferns of matter
beside the dam of water – flatter
than the sea which has wind —
to blow the flames.

People are burning their souls in their fires,
from out of their chimneys comes smoke.
TV is burning their eyes and their brain.
Brown bricks crumble – and the people?
They collapse.

Mother gives sweeties to Robert.
(Will he throw himself on the railway line?)
Father's not puzzled –
four pints he's just guzzled
and Robert's not his, anyway –
Today!

[These words were also used as part of the track 'From An Electric Train' on the LP 'A Raise Of Eyebrows' (Transatlantic STRA 161)]

On stage at the Bolton Festival, 1979/08/29

Train Travellers pre 1974 *Fallables p.35*

Sunlight flickered through the trees
upon the almost eyes of train travellers.

Limp bodies
flop around
and finger nails are most important,
as are specks on suits
and turned-up
turned-down
stitched-out
stitched-in
trouser-leg coverings.

Do not forget
the tie adjustment procedure,
the cuff aspect,
and the almost eyes of train travellers.

Turmoil pre 1970 *Fallables p.99*

My head's in a turmoil!

Why can't I take it off
and rest it awhile
on someone's mantelpiece?

Cos the mantelpiece is well taken up
with the supporting of toy dogs.

Twist late 1960s

A twisted, knarled and naked tree claws upwards out of its plush green surroundings to grasp the meaning of air and get away from the ever-encroaching human rubbish. But all he might grasp are the wires from an electricity pylon – which would be his downfall..

Some young and straight colleagues, looking like feathers stuck in the ground, have been formed up along a road. And where are they leading? Where are they leading? To an enormous cement works featuring much corrugated metal and such.

And the other tree can't decide whether to grip the electric wires or not.

Two Feet And A Mouth 1971/2

[To be performed, seated, heavily tapping a regular beat (with some half-beats, heel-and-toeing) with a reasonably heavy pair of shoes.]

Two feet tapped to show the way.
Two hands waved to show the play
and, "This way, that way, weave your thing –
make your pattern, not just sing.
Thrust your thought about the ring
where ropes are sparks and back they fire
to thrust your thought through sticky mire
of people reading newspapers —
fusepapers —
refuse sheets, Daily Bleats.
And is the World to be,
and not bounce on Mao's knee
for who's he, who's he, who's he, who's he —

"Footballers grow hair that's long
to show that they do not belong
in common places, pop stars' faces!"
"Who star-gazes?" *[shout]*

All of us, so make no fuss.
It's looking for that better place
in brain of cheese and moon of face,
in hands in pockets, eyes in sockets,
feet in fist! "Contortionist!!"

"Gossip, gossip, my friend's fine!"
Her mother's not. She took the line
that I was bad and not too good
and would not invite me for food,
not even scones! That's what she should
have placed on circles on a plate
for us to argue 'pon my fate
and "Whose friend's whose?" and "That's not right!"
and "Don't come shouting here at night!"
and "That's not proper. Cut that caper.
'Tis not written in newspaper."
"Whose paper??!!!" *[huge shout]*

Write your stuff upon the sky
cos then you step back with your eye
and view the matter.

Shapely clouds will come along
and clear all that, and that's not wrong
cos then you'll find another place
to write your stuff – keep up the pace
of fertile mind (The Output Race) –
so Mrs. Brown took off her face.

For every thought that is ejected,
new ones are to be expected.
Clear out all those old thoughts now,
keep your head your life-force. "How??!!!" *[huge shout]*

By — *[here you have to finish with rhythmically improvised phonetics until exhausted]*

Waiting For Life 1972

The twitching, pulsing, hairy, mal-formed thing that wriggled on the waiting-room floor, sniffed and slobbered with its tongue protruding intermittently in truly obscene suggestions.

    The male half of its owner, who had a similar mouth and eyes, flicked ash from his cigarette remarkably close to its bulbous eyes and barked orders at it to cover the sound of ash on eyeball. It snuffled loudly, like trying to propel record-sized bogeys a record distance.

    Its female owner had a funny hat on, but this was no doubt from a reputable milliners. She started to kiss the hairy thing with her long nose. This made the bogey projections much more violent, and then quieter, as the sound was taken over with grinding teeth and paw-on-floor scraping.

    The pet, domestic, lovable dog was loved, domestically and lovably, and they all lived together – discussing the unreliability of the weather and the public transport.

[Performed on the album 'As He Stands' RON28]

Walking 1971

It's a strange thing, walking and seeing one's shoes clip clop flashing, slip slop clashing – laces waving in the breeze among taut-strapped ankles – one of the few things left to jangle free about the human person. How big and fat the shoes look from one's own head viewpoint – how slim and neat, flat-placed on street they look when seen in a shop window or other mirror device.

Turned-in toes are for those not desiring to progress much in thought or journey.

Widdle 1975/12/–

My bladder, sandwiched in my crossed legs, complained deeply about holding up two pints of Mr. Young's Finest Real Bitter. From my view point in the full-width 2nd Class section, I wondered what little rooms lay off the 1st Class corridor.

As the train and several other people's liquid intake proceeded southwards through the night, I watched with much interest one or two fellow 2nd Classers edge their predicament down the 1st Class corridor in search of the little hole to the granite chips, but each returned with just enough gray-faced cover-up smile to ensure the continuing flow.

I considered relaxing, I considered pulling the little red chain, leaping out at every next station, or quietly depositing a puddle on the seat (as would some little folk in their first year primary school class) but, by the time I had forced my brain round that lot, every man but one had left the carriage and no doubt had already experienced the round, warm, tingling sensation of projecting his load down some green-stained station porcelain or perishing the rubber of someone else's tyre in the carpark.

My only chance was to hope that there was nobody in one of the 1st Class compartments. Boldly nearly standing up, twitchingly adjusting my scarf to notice that the other man wasn't looking, I got into the nearest compartment. Due to British Rail's low volts and watts, I painlessly removed the two light bulbs with my bare hands so that I could not be seen by any totally unconcerned Sussex wayfarers, or totally concerned old ladies with telescopes, pulled down the window, which is really half-up at best, and experimented on tip-toes to see if my hose would stretch over it, all the while looking round to check if I was discovered, not for any of the obvious reasons but for having unlawful intercourse with fresh air! All was quiet, so the side of the carriage got its first spray wash for ages.

What are the aerodynamics of pee? Would the man further up the train find horizontal rain on a clear frosty night a bit unusual?

Well, nobody knew, or cared, it would seem, but the flexible human had won again over the ill-equipped machine.

Wind Of Life 1966

The wind blew – in Marylebone Station.

> The people stood – or walked,
> till they could find a place to stand.
> They were very glum.

> The engine has not appeared.

> The statues move – occasionally.

> Wind – blows – cold — nearly.

> Negro porters argue upon another platform furiously.

> Nobody knows anybody else.

> We all get on the train.

> All is quiet – and warm.

> Two more people get in and let in the wind which blows – cold — nearly.

> Will these people never stop getting in and letting in the wind?

> The grand finale seems to be the rustling of newspapers – and throats.

Have you a newspaper – to join the men from the office sitting in clusters of newspapers and striped ties? The barbers' trade still makes money from these people! Have you patronised the barbers' trade?
    Black toe-capped shoes amuse the eye which has observed the silent symphonic composition of newspapers – and they're not important newspapers, but they've got nice short easy paragraphs and pictures, preliminaries, in fact, for the screen of British Life which will whine and flicker later in the evening and cause the black toe-capped shoes to gleam – and whine and flicker – and cause the wife to whine and flicker, and flick her soul of inner being three inches short of the eight foot high ceiling which is the living room.

[as child] "Daddy, what is life?"

"Oh, that's the symphonic poem of the train and the newspapers conducted by the suspended black toe-capped shoes. The wind creeps in somewhere, but it's not intended."

Wrong Line 1971/2

"Now is the time for lifting the roof off!"

A man almost stirred in the corner.

"Whose problem?"

Next to me skulks a shadow of me and it's not much of any use. Painted fingernails read a book. Spectacles sleep and tired blinking eyes read the cover of the painted fingernails.

Thus did the railway carriage disappear up its own dirty pendant curtains. Shadows of people's reflections nearly reflected but merged away into twilight hedges.

"Blast!" I nearly shouted, and a coat waved at me from a luggage rack.

"SShhh!" I nearly whispered, and the bowels of the train's rumbling rumbled up again – covering my presentation of a fart of garlic and fresh cream, collected from an Italian restaurant in that throat of London, the Charing Cross Road.

"**Ici Gatwick!**"

"I'm on the wrong line of train!"

On stage at the Third Eye Centre, Glasgow, 1979/09/01

A Brisk Walk Out 1971   *Fallables p.53*

Mr Postman scluff your heels.
Try to see how Pavement feels.
Big dogs, small dogs squat and strain
on the Pavement! – miss the drain.
Spit and gob on Pavement grey.
I'm off to grass and there to stay!

A Revelous Fellow pre 1970   *Fallables p.14*

A revelous fellow, with brain made of yellow,
came down from the clouds one day.
"Good God!" he said and, with dismay,
"I've never even met the fellow!"
So he crossed himself and went away.

Two years later, and several days,
the man who had the yellow ways
popped up from the ground, making lots of sound,
bowed to the nearest Government
and rushed off to the Underground,
where he got cemented in –
of course!

A Twisted Tree pre 1974   *Fallables p.2*

A twisted tree reached up for air,
its crippled branches flailing there.
Its bark was gone quite long ago
but it's still there, out of its row,
out of its life, out of its death,
but there no less – and breathing breath.

Almost Nearly early 1970s

Almost nearly? – Was it really?
Where it went? – Has it gone?
Did it live to see most clearly
foggy brightness shone?

Did it see to live most dearly,
reaching heights and falling down,
rising up to stand mid-way,
telling wind it would not sway
in the lights – a mottled clown?

Hiding wares from prying eyes
in plastic see-through bag of lies,
bouncing glares off see-through eyes,
its frame a wind-bag full of sighs,
its name a faithful horse that shies.

Come on! Really nearly clearly!
I'll guide you if you'll guide me.
Splosh through puddles, splashed with muddles –
"Come on, this way! – Can't you see?"
"Now we're both lost! – Let me free!"
"See you next year. Come for tea,
phoning first – might not be free.
(Your moaning thirst will not sway me.)"

"It always was – for nearly ever –
living lives in other's skins.
Flashing knives and skinning friendships –
cover-wearer always wins."
Always? Always?? Clearly nearly.
Really clearly almost wins.
Clearly almost dearly wins.
Wins? Wins?? Clearly nearly.
Almost clearly nearly dearly.
Almost nearly dearly clearly . . . . . *[for ever]*

Back Britain 1967

The world is a green banana,
for that's what you shall eat,
wrapped up in a bag marked 'Britain'
which is certainly not on heat,
cos paper bags with Union Jacks
do nothing to shift the mound
of fat legged ladies on buses with groceries –
(By Jove! That's very compound!)
but not as compound as living
which seems very difficult now,
caused by people who're "Backing Britain"
waving Union Jacks, and a cow.
What's that got to do with it anyway? –
It would all seem a bit of a drag,
but you try when you're out shopping
to hold milk in a paper bag.

Bag Of Love 1972

On stage
at the Third
Eye Centre,
Glasgow,
1979/09/01

"I've brought my bag of love for you."
　　　　　　　　"Just put it over there."
"Aren't you going to see how much?"
　　　　　　　　"No, I've no time to spare."

Bath Oil Thankyou 1989/12/27

I've tried this oil upon my bath
and even whisked the foam,
but buttocks against porcelain
will squeak till cows come home.

I've tried this oil upon my head
to replace hair I lack,
but now I've found my hair has slipped
just further down my back.

I've sent some oil to Bath for fun,
to test the waters there
and soon got message, "Mixed in glass
makes zoider zlip down fair!"

So here I am, just out of bath,
still all bald with squeaks,
a-standing in the garden fair,
freshly towelled and still quite bare,
coyly posed in Sussex air,
a rose among the leeks.

Bon Fire 1975

On old grey earth a bonfire burns
and three old men hunch round.
Their glowing orange jackets say
they're not so frail and not so pale
but sometimes work for British Rail,
but not much more today.

Bow-Tie Thankyou 1991/01/17

[The bow-tie was made from a textile printed with part of a French road map.]

Ho! Ho! Mon Dieu! Ce n'est pas juste!
Un papillon that's just been loosed,
erratic flutter East and West,
its own routes printed on its vest.

I do intend to wear this thing
and leap and dive and growl and sing.
I'll go to France when it's quite hot
and spin with bow-tie on the spot.

No need for reeling drinking bout,
I bow to this tie's sorting out
the routes that freely dislocate
fixed planning, scowling round a plate.
Indeed, 'tis chance that's grasped so sound
through bow-tie that makes *you* spin round.

Brain-Twirl 1973

Whose brain is this that twirls around?
Whose feet are these that clear the ground?
Are they the knees that ache and grind?
Are these the eyes, joined to the mind
that whirls and tips itself around
and makes the feet float off the ground?
Are these the eyes that ache and grind,
and flood, through noticing mankind
in posh machines with poses queer,
with back-lit light to show quite clear
its nakedness and blemish twisted?
Surely not! My eyes are misted!

I'll blink – that is the common cure –
but who am I to be so sure
with brain that beats and twirls around
and misses beats with feet off ground?
And, which am I in modern race
where nobody quite finds his place,
where everybody poses strange
to make his mark – within his range –
and shows his teeth, which soon drop out
(from weary worry – there's no doubt!).
Ah now, there I go again!
You cannot call it 'slip of pen'
'cos bleating brain controls all that,
which really puts me on the mat –
placed carefully by salesman slick,

seducing weak-willed buyer, sick
from being shrunk little, trousers trodden,
neck all wet and brain all sodden.

But here I stop lest I get bitter –
tell you what produced this twitter.

Here I sit inside a plane
with hot meal clad in cellophane.
Savory biscuit caught me napping –
can't get cheese out from its wrapping.

Britain Is Great 1970s

Britain is great for being grated
and battered by waves on all shores –
where workers wave back with two fingers
and drowned in official downpours.

But out of this turmoil of splashing –
this inside-out pond for the free –
come birds made of hide, computers inside
for setting their courses around the world wide –
Good Greatness! Must dash – and be me.

By The Sea 1971

I'm a fishingman's daughter from Grimsby Town.
I don't have a dress or a posh evening gown.
I've got hair down my back, but more on my chest.
I'm a real proper mermaid and one of the best.

Cards Thankyou 1989/12/29

Happy Families are rare –
the cards, collectors seek.
Just peep behind new-painted door,
just look at clothes upon the floor,
just feel the noise of tempers sore
to know of what I speak.

The thing about this new-made pack
is that they're *never* happy
being in clusters all the same –
they've never cast off nappy.

A happy family looks out
at many things precarious
and each participant goes out
and brings back contrasts various.

If teachers, peace campaigners, clowns,
all stuck in separate houses,
they'd soon go rotten, seek to change
and wriggle up Gays' blouses!!

They've wriggled bloody far enough –
I see them all too clear –
but thanks for cards to crystallise
my thoughts this time of year.

Chrisfarce 1972

In my head, Christmas enters by this ear,
but passes through to leave me clear
for slow evolvement, year by year –
world-wound revolvement without fear.

But fear there is at back of mind
for them that's made to be unkind –
the kind that elbows those complete
off glitt'ry way – 'long Oxford Street –
to enter shop to buy a boot
which, after Christmas, rots off foot.

Yes, Christmas comes without a cheer,
without a smile, more like a leer
from banker's vaults in which we've drowned
with sweat from petty, papered Pound.

Jingle bells and down the chute
comes money bartered for that boot,
comes honey used to oil the wheels
of finance, fat men (pigs' throat squeals).
"He send a card. I sent him none.
I see that something must be done.
To corner shop! Get dearer one!
It's only that that makes it fun."

It's only that that makes me run
down shady lanes to find the sun –
to find a spark not seen in face
of those who're in the Bond Street race.
Look out who bends to tie his lace!
Splosh! Into gutter – bus-tyre's place.

Bus conductors seem all right
with ringside seat to watch the fight
'twixt man and men who choose to play
the Christmas game the money way.

Now, on to food and eating that,
and eating others who're too fat.
"Who'll wash the dishes?" loud, you shout.
"Which relative will help us out?" –
to save us all being bored to tea
with Auntie Flossie, waxing free
'pon subjects clean, domestic chat
and where she'll buy her next new hat.
So, when you wrap your Christmas parcel,
write thereon: "Merry Chrisfarcel".

God's Son? God's Teeth! God's knees as well!
The whole lot's fallen down the well.
The bucket's jammed, the rope's just broken –
I hope somebody shouts, "Well spoken!"

Confession late 1960s

I'm pleased Mummy noticed the marks on the mirror
'cos I've been wanting to confess
that fried bread, fats and cooked amazements
cause spots which, when squeezed, make a terrible mess.

Doors 1970s – completed 1993/10/10

Do you know the secret
of how to open doors?

I charged at one – it slid right past.
I heaved at one – it stuck quite fast.
I stared at one – it never closed.
I kicked at one, to find exposed
a room of twenty-three green chairs
and, on each seat, a tuft of hairs
since paint had just been freshly done
and fluffy cat had tried each one.

A shadow crept across the floor
that led my eyes to see what more
this still-life box could keep from me
so, gently dropping on one knee,
I sensed a glow from near-left wall
and glimpsed a dribbly painted scrawl
right next to green-eyed corpse on floor
who'd swallowed brush, but not before
he'd solved his problem on the spot
and drowned the cat in green paint pot.

Fashion 1971/2

Mrs. Brown took off her grey,
to keep it for another day,
and chose her green for to be seen
against her pink accessory.

It did not quite do all it should
so she brought out her yellow hood
to hide her head, which was quite bare
from worrying what to wear just there.

She hid her eyes from more surprise
with purple silk, made just to size,
in case she blushed from feeling wrong
or crows-feet showed and got too long.
So, swathed in things of divers cloth,
she chanced upon a quite-big moth
which ate her clothes and stripped her bare
and left her lying rotting there.

Film pre 1974   *Fallables p.71*

"I want to make a film!" he said
and picked his nose into his head.

Said I, "First learn to blink the eye
and look about, perhaps the sky,
perhaps a cow about to shit
with tail erect, perhaps a pit
that's dug by men
who work all day from ten to ten to ten again
and not much pay do they get then."

So, make the most of all the land
and then perhaps we'll understand –

why ladies powder nose on trains.

On stage at the Bolton
Festival, 1979/08/29

For Katie Hewitt – aged 9 1988/07/23

Let water run between your toes,
let rain run through your hair,
let friends and foes show how it goes,
let cross old ladies twitch their nose,
let clothes hang loose,
let chocolate mousse
a-trickle down the stair.

A-bang, a-boo and Gawd knows what,
a pudding on your head,
a-grumble bumble stagger stumble –
now it's time for bed.

For Sale 1974/03/–

I have for sale a twisted thought
which eats me up and can't be bought –
exhudes from head to foot of head
and makes me restless when in bed.

Sweet honeysuckle twists around
to get its leaves and flowers off ground
so human's foot can't stand on it,
but here comes tractor, puffing shit,
and look what it's got on its roof –
a metal whirling disc – forsooth!

For more than that! It's come to see
that honeysuckle wrenched out, free
to wither, wilt and curl up dry.
What have I said? What chance have I?

Geesin's An Odd Name early 1970s

I'm really not the son of Gee
or "Gee, him! Geesim", "Guess who? Gessin."
There's no Z where S should be
nor Easton, Esson, Goosin, Gettim!
G is hard as 'grope' or 'goo' –
I'm naughty Ron Gee*sin*, that's who.

Ron as The Consultant for friends' retirement surprise

Gone – But Nearly There 1982/07/02

[written during film shoot of Scotch Myths]

I tried to share my soul with yours
and put it in your bag
but found you'd pulled the string too tight
so soul got squashed while in mid-flight.
I went through shaky void that night –
a bumpy fluttered drag.

You shed a tear when pulling string.
I thought, "Ah, waters flow! –
a healthy shower before a swim –
a rippled massage for each limb!" –
diverted though to steaming gym,
a sporting complex blow.

I followed you through tubes and glass
and strained up bars and ropes,
just free enough to see the glow
of sun-lit flickered pool below,
but fearing then to plunge too low
and rip out ling'ring hopes.

So, hurting there in tangled rope,
I swung and spun in pain
and watched your careful formed descent
down bars well fixed with strong cement.
I screamed a mute, "This was not meant!"
but rope just twirled again.

Your long and steady pushing stride
left wispy marks on door –
a far-planned exit from the fear
of my being near to see you clear
It's true your blue eyes squeezed a tear,
but I was gushing more.

You were not there to see all this,
which made me all the sadder.
I missed your gentle sparkling gaze
reflecting talk of finding ways
of showing other routes from maze
of Britain's Broken Bladder.

At this, I sent you my odd rhyme
saying, "Think you're mad? – I'm madder!"
I've now had half a day to wonder
(aided much by Wagner's thunder)
if your head is split asunder
or just rendered sadder.

I really hope we meet again
to grin at my emotion,
to free our strangled guarded joy,
dispense with playground game and ploy
and, like some harmless playroom toy,
not kick it while in motion.

These olde-fashioned bumpy lines
which are my thoughts right now
should give a lead to my unrest –
a patchy, splashing, puddled quest –
a struggling scrambling for the best –
a laughing, screaming row!

By now, if you're not smiling on,
we're nearly there as friends, but gone.

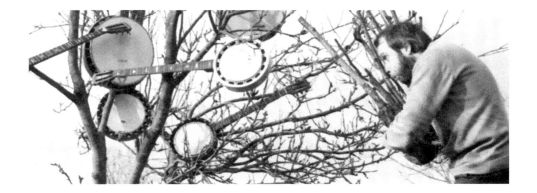

Ron with tree-root bagpipes
and banjo tree, 1972/02/–

Grated Britain mid 1970s

Grated Britain smells of curry.
What do you think of that?
I know a man who's in a hurry –
smells like his old cat.

I've seen a lady – smells of roses –
thorns emerge from eyes.
Grated Britain smells of cabbage,
rotting in its lies.

Squirt another fragrance sweetheart,
squeeze a tube of styles,
see those noses nuzzle nowhere –
running metric miles.

Onward sideways, smell the burning!
What can you do 'bout that?
Shrieking workers, arms out wideways,
put us on the mat.
Harmful shirkers, down the slideways –
running out of flat.

Grated Britain hides away
in underventilated nest.
Smell the noise of hibernation.
Hear the pulse of pure stagnation.
Write a sign across the nation:
"Britain stands – in holey vest."

Clutching parts that folks can't reach,
smearing oil from weeping beach.
Pissed newsreader slips and slides,
hanging onto job like leech.

"Ah Ha! Oh No! He He, Ho Ho!"
shout the people in their hurry,
"What do we do to make our minds grow?
How do we see when we can't? We're so low.
Let's apply for a grant – remain so
we can smell of British Curry."
(I'm optimistic – please don't worry.)

Houses 1967

Silhouetted houses
black against the sky
frowning down on humans
who might dare to pass by.

Pretty little faces,
undisturbed as yet,
smile very sweetly –
soon they'll forget
what it's like to feel
all warm inside
cos the houses have engulfed them!

But all they've got to worry 'bout
is the colour of the walls
in the nasty black houses!

And as their brains darken
and their chimneys pour forth soot,
their 20 watt bulbs flicker
and they begin to put
their souls in their fires
and pollute the atmosphere,
and here – and here – and here – and here –

On stage at the Third Eye Centre, Glasgow, 1979/09/01

I've Never Come This Way Before 1976
[Recorded in multi-voices as 'Hiding haul of voices, hail!' on the album 'Right Through' RON323]

I've never come this way before
revolving intermittent
door through which we seek to
learn to find our balanced
mind you do it's good for
you are not so good for
you are sometimes someone
else you're late with thought on
plate of steel all bent round
head that way no maybe
this is better calmer
even when the mind is
round a twisted bend or
two ears still to take in
waves of clouds mist over
eyes all sore with dark
discerning learning under
ground in coffee grinder's
lid lifts off for some or
else he's got his tongue stuck
out for solitary
joy of being well wedged in
door through which we seek to
burn our letters to our
soul's on fire and wind's up
grate of learning through which
fall some ashes bent nails
bits of half charred woody
crusts of wonder dust of
thunder claps the brain-shout
effort more than pipes with
standing on a wind-pipe's
jacket torn and pocket's
gone to tailor standing
there he's threadbare thought-squeezed
through his needle's eye it
went from thence still ringing
bell with clapper cracking
shell of dapper dwelling
place your money odds on
square that's dropped right through the

board of substance-thought quite
sound investigation
pending infestation
trial of human's brain in
jar of pickle out we
climb up wall with patterned
carpet sideways gripping
feet march blisteringly
on round lightbulb pulsing
power off generators
wheels of other people's
learning fast revolving
faster round the globe I
go to stop the print says
long life lights your way to
death's not come I'm upside
down on ceiling leaping
faster off this long life
scorching souls that march on
effort leaps across the
ceiling cracks but does not
break this stubborn human
scrape across to door on
hinges squeaky staying
open intermittent
door through which we leak to
yearn for learning bullets
fire through synchronously
fashioned glossy door blades
flashing faster than we
see our bullets propelled
safely out to foggy
thought world still revolving
always smiling moon face
caught whirls spiral spinning
onward cleaving structures
complex molecules of
matter not what's done
I've never gone this way before
behind a rainbow-clouded door,
in front of thought and reason clear,
an opaque prism scrambles here
and leaves us new stuff, holes of matter.
"Silence now! Just hear the clatter!"

Cogs of thought and thought of cogs
bring me down to man with clogs
who, dancing with his beer in hand,
breaks the glass while trying to land,
releases gas, glass cuts his hand
    and he becomes –
        first –
        man –
    unmanned.

Jane & Mike Fond Do 1987/12/12

Great Jane and Mike and Matthew and Will,
I've writ this wee poem to youse up the hill
for Saturday's night of the year at your place
with ne'r a dull glassful and ne'r a straight face,
where thoughts full of chuckles blurped keenly from pot
and feelings of life at its best cooked up hot.
A colourful, artfuly-staged orchestration,
a glorious passion to dispel frustration!
In the race for festivities, here are my views:
We'll all have to go some so Christmas won't lose!

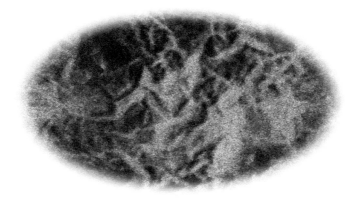

Lockdown 2020/06/07

I'm getting pissed in the sunset,
propped up in a grey garden chair,
outside of the house during lockdown
and glad that there's nobody there.

I'm riddled with Chattering Classes –
they gush out from Radio Four:
"This is right!" "No, that's left!" "Where's the centre?"
"No more!" I say, "Please, no more!"

The roses are blooming and waving.
The sunshade is clapping the breeze.
The crows and the magpies are squawking
with more sense than any of these.

Technology helped us to travel
and visit the splendours abroad,
then planes returned laden
with bugs that were made in
a place that should be outlawed.

So now we're all battered and buggered,
we turn to the scientists, skilled
in finding a vaccine quite quickly
before we all end up quite killed.

Lying In Bed c. 1973

Aaahh! Shooting pain of indigestion
wakes me up to ask the question,
"What do I not realise
while blinking thinking with closed eyes?"

But I lie staring 'cross the snow,
see sun and moon together glow
in rare and embryonic light
pulling day up out of night
and, blinking at my lady's eyes,
I find myself uncompromise –
and nudge and nestle, with some power,
to celebrate this early hour.

"It's nearly February, Dear,
and time to start our own New Year!"

It must be time to struggle out –
put on our skin and leap about –
put on our voice to shout out loud,
"Lying in bed is not allowed!"

Down the stairs our boys are bumping
answering the postman's thumping.
Is this Christmas second rising?
No, just creepy advertising.

Still, the boys are stirred awake
with kitchen clatter. Cupboards shake.
Up they bump and thump with tray
to splash our minds with tea, and say,
"It must be time to struggle out –
put on your skin and leap about –
put on your voice to shout out loud,
'Lying in bed is not allowed!'"

Pedal organ down below
moans bits from Smurfs and Greasy show,
but it's bits from Mozart's fun
that banish moon and crown the sun –
force us out from steaming bed
to start the New Year in our head.

But think on this, it must be said:
all this thought while lying in bed.

Man Of Business 1971

A man of business looked at me,
his brows he raised to make him see.
Could he not just look quite plain
instead of raising eyes again?

His shoes were waxed, and polished too,
designed with thought to dazzle you.
"Which part of you?" you cry in vain.
It's all for eyebrows, raised again.
His transportation is the train,
his legs are crossed like rigid crane,

his eyes are fixed in rigid brain,
he studies papers, writ quite plain
with numbers, figures, mostly black,
with red pen notes, avoiding sack –
avoiding green and purple too:
"That's garish, Ted, and just won't do!"
his boss cries out, to reach for phone
through which he sings 'The Business Drone':
"Cut back, cut back, economise!
Now, toilet rolls, the standard size
should be the tissue paper stiff
and not that posh pink perfumed whiff!"

Those of you, aware of touch
will realise that twice as much
of that old tissue-tearing crinkle
is used up for bum and winkle –
also causes arse to wrinkle.
What did they use before that?
Why, good old grass – I lift my hat!
I haven't got one, never mind.
The human race continues blind
that progress isn't always kind
to skin and hands and 'Dip them in'
and throw your polythene in bin
to be transported by dustmen
who dump the same in rubbish pen,
but this is blown o'er fence and fen
to give the trees those plastic leaves
that decorate suburban eaves –
along with plaster-casted cat
that rests on roof-tiles. Fancy that!
No, not even plastic gnomes
that decorate the front of homes,
nor Christmas trees, seasonal fuss,
when they're young firs required by us
to grow up tall and straight and wide
to show us Life is on our side.

The human brain needs space to think
and food to breathe and air to drink.

And all man-made dwellings and towns and erections
sometimes, quite often, make us lose directions.

Message 1987/01/22

Dialogue, Dye-a-log, Dial-a-log in
to the Grate fireplace and make a big din.
Fizzle and Fuzzle and cackle with fun –
amuse *ONESELF*, and then everyone.

Mini Liquid Golf Game Thankyou 1991/01/29

I've stood in rough, I've stood on tee,
I've wrapped my club right round a tree,
I've played in sun, I've played in rain,
gone out of bounds down farmer's lane,
been up to ears in bunker's hole
and stubbed a club in house of mole
and chewed my way up Club's flagpole.
Oh, crazy golfing me!

But now I've stopped to prune fruit trees,
enjoying Sunday morning breeze.
No more posing on the course
with ear being bent by partner's force.
Now I can sit in soft seclusion,
puzzling out your golf illusion,
coming to the hard conclusion:
It's a bloody tease!

I twist to left, I twist to right,
I nearly hurl it out of sight.
I stand on foot, I stand on head,
but getting nine balls in their bed
is just as hard a golfing game
but here's solution that I claim:
This liquid biscuit takes the blame
so I will take a bite!

Monks Green Farm (An Imaginary History) 1993/12/23

[for dear friends, living at Fetcham, Leatherhead.]

Atop a knoll, by Leatherhead, in Surrey's land, unsung
arrived a monk in quest of ale to quench his cloistered tongue.
A dropping, drooping friar he was 'til comely wench came near.
"Ah, Sire, what Leather Head you are – I'm in the work of beer
and jugs have I and foaming pots and diverse vessels plenty."
"Well Fetcham lass, afore I die, for those I must soon em'ty!
And have you hid in fireplace wide a bit of ham, well smoky?
Well, fetch that too for that'll fuel us for our hokey-cokey."

A right fine wench she was indeed, with plenty dumplings boiling
and mechanisms churning well – that sometimes wanted oiling.
So, off she trundles to the sound of yonder Friar's lips
a-licking smacking in elation, viewing her buxom hips.

At Leatherhead, a fair while later, Jenny Green puffed in
to check her brew, a lush dark bitter, foaming in the bin.
She climbed up high on shaky steps, majestic o'er the brim,
but ample dumplings, plus the fumes, tipped Jenny for a swim.

Well-oiled she got, and full right well, imbibing more than ration.
A fool was she to be so keen for Monk whose fashion's passion.
And sunk was she, claimed by the brew, consumed as nutriment –
the yeast frothed wildly o'er the brim, an amber firmament.

The glow was spied by Monk on knoll who gasped, "My love's right fired!"
and panted fresh for ale and flesh until he near expired
but news soon spread of yeasty grave that wholly did her harm.
He gasped his last and fertilised the site of Monk's Green Farm.

Nice Old Lady pre 1974   *Fallables p.21*

Nice old lady with your leg done round –
elastic bandage holding sound –
regular rhythm of the train wheels' feet –
spectacle-case tap-tap quite neat.
Posture pleasing, eyes outside

noticing trees in breeze beside,
quietly changing head around
brown fur hat is mole's earth mound.
Wonder where blind mole is now?
Does he know of Human's row?
Click clack rush roar – train speeds on,
nice old lady on your sit-upon
swaying gently, never flustered
little lace hankie, fingers clustered
tap little beat out – forefinger key
sensing smooth skin, not like me!
I'm always searching, never finding
your knowledge nodding, never minding.
I'm driving on to the train's roar beat,
you'll tap your years out – comfy seat.

Here we go then – through our eye,
I'll take the whippy hedge, you take the sky.

Little lace foot tap – gone quite pleasantly.
I'll run to catch up – get there presently.

No Doubt Influenced By Spike Milligan late 1960s

When your brain is turning to jelly
and it's running out your ears,
put some cotton wool in
and live a few more years.

For life is good for you, and you,
even if your car is not,
so put some cotton wool in
and put an end to the rot.

People, whizzing about like mad,
their cars are all aflame.
The car tyre firms are not so sad
but they're partly to blame –
by causing pseudo-humans to think
they're coming to grips with the road —
BANG!

Nutcracker Thankyou 1989/12/27

Dear James's, (Evelyn, George and Neil),
"A nut-cracker's nut crack?
Another one?" I thought at first,
but soon my crack changed tack.

Most tools for nuts have steely grip
and wrong-sized jaws for shell,
so when, with sherry, folk desire
a nutty nibble round the fire,
they wrench and squeeze and fair perspire
and blow their bits to hell!

But your wee tool is cup and screw,
a-crafted from best tree,
much nearer to the nut's own root
(on end of branch it hung as fruit),
it even dropped down at your foot –
then screwed to death with glee!

Nut's on its bike, it's past the lips,
it's mangled by the jaw,
its cycle chain's all buggered up –
fell foul of Christmas law.

O'er Precipice 1969/1993

"Ninety-six! Yes, ninety-six!"
"How many bricks?" "Well, six."
"What do humans do with these?"
"Tricks, mere tricks, just tricks."

Little boys throw them at trains
and parents say, "My! 'Ees got brains.
Defends 'imself at any cost.
We won't let our son be bossed,
'cept by us 'oo belt 'im round
an' grind 'is 'ead into the ground –
fuck me if teacher don't come round
to check if all our 'eads is sound!"

"Course they is!" they always say.
"Don't we bring 'ome some right good pay?"
No love, or other allied stuff,

which makes their son become 'right tough'.
And when he gets his home of bricks –
more, lots more than ninety-six –
gangrene notes give him his kicks,
and put him back to when he's six.
He buys a car, its bulging sheen
reminds him clear of where it's been.
He buried one in playschool sand,
(He made it fly to make it land.)
so now he's big, with mouth and pay,
he dials on carphone, splutters spray,
"Hey Mummy! Mummy! Look at this!"
and drives it clean o'er precipice.

On Cooking Roast Pork, Braised Onions & Fresh Runner Beans – With A Bottle Of Red Wine – For The Cook And Author (the same)
1994/09/15

Chiddle-chaddle, shiddle-shaddle,
Dumpy doodly plonkit.
Piddle-paddle, diddle-daddle,
Skippety oobly donkit.

It tasted fine. My belted line
is hanging o'er the vest.
So, "Bugger I," says man on earth,"
God's in the pan – that's best."

On Visiting A Middle-Class Aspect pre 1974   *Fallables p.44*

Corrugated, half truncated
brains of nearly being
pester me about this time
as I do search another line
or up a pole do try to climb
to aid some people's seeing.

By Jove, or God, or Christ knows who!
I'm pinioned here in some old zoo
with cups, and saucers, up my flue!
What will it come for me to do?
Get back to Sussex, quick, the noo
in choo choo train, "Whooo-woo-ha who?"
Me.

One Pair Of Eyes pre 1974   *Fallables p.58*

A sweaty pair of eyes looked out
at many things advancing
to pluck them from their sockets
and set their brain a-dancing.

A-dancing off the boot
of shorn-haired trousered foot,
off long-haired shredded pockets,
off regimented boot.

To meet their destination,
yes, turn around and face it,
of concrete brains and plastic feet
and ladders up your facelift.
Ropes tied to ears and rings to hands
and humans gathering in bands
of light and shade and darkness blind,
that thing that does upset the mind
and causes plucked eyeballs to find
a home of sorts in gutter deep –
a sludge-filled hall in which to sleep
for ever on and nearly ever.

Oriental Food Thankyou 1989/12/29

A Cache of oriental taste
and Bombay Duck's strong savour!
The Yin and Yang that's ne'r the same
o'er hills and dales of flavour.

You've ventured out and chanced your choice,
a move I pat on back –
a new thing found, a new day round –
you'll never richness lack.
But, faced with packets exotique,
I need *another* book
for rehydration formulation
leading on to cook.

A year ago you sent to me
a pack of black fungi.
I wet it and was soon engulfed
by bloated octopi.

So on we go in wide-eyed shout,
"Encourage salivation!
The heart of stomach is the place
to top Christian salvation!"

Page Watcher pre 1974 *Fallables p.3*

Hello, hello, it's me again.
I'm writing with a felt-tip pen.
Why am I writing? I'm not sure.
Maybe I've got word allure.

"What's word allure?" they ask again.
It's writing with a felt-tip pen
and watch it squiggle 'cross the page
and watch grey hairs fall out with age
and watch the wind blow 'cross the page
and watch the page go brown with age.

Someone'll preserve it, never you fear,
to drag its corpse out year by year
and clog a brain or two quite hard
and coat an ear or two with lard.

It's freshness! – that's the thing to get,
so now read on and don't forget.

Patterned Hankies Thankyou 1991/01/16

Hello again, it's me for sure
projecting cerebral manure
with thankyou card a bit delayed
by life and things that are Ron-made.

So, thank you for the dot, dot, dot
(a-carried on two cloths for snot),
the patterns will disguise a lot
allowing me to mop and blot.

We had a lovely Chrisfarce –
I thought it would not end.
I must propose that date be moved
to suit nearest weekend.

Two ducks we ate twice-toured the world,
reduced our teeth to gum,
and turkey spent the last 6 months
with hosepipe up its bum!

So now it's war on rabbits –
they're gnawing at our trees.
I'm going to give them something
that'll bring them to their knees,
bring them to the cooking pot
with cider, herbs and fat shallot.
I'll whisper gently, "That's yer lot,
we'll have your flavour, please".
(So, with the pepper and your cloths,
I'll have a damn good sneeze.)

Relief 1976

When I'm feeling all harassed
and nearly on my knees,
I gets into a nice hot bath
and lies right back – and pees.

Ron's Address 1994/01/23

*[Written to introduce the 'Hystery' CD collection of 28 years of work –
read over the rhythmic hammering in of a huge wooden post in the garden.]*

We are climbing over fences
and we're crawling over mounds
while we scratch our itchy senses
and then pamper them with sounds.

We are going down a tunnel
and we're in an aeroplane,
but we think that all this fun'll
drive us pretty well insane.

But we surf across an ocean
and we scramble through a gate,
often with intense emotion,
shaking organs into motion,
(inflammation soothed with lotion)
no doubt getting in a state.

Wheeled along in builder's barrow,
skating upside down on head,
shows us that our vision's narrow
and our nerves have gone quite dead.

So we soar across a hill or two
and pause upon a tree
to look down on the human zoo
that's made by you, and me.

But, really, really, stated clearly,
I love this the best.
I love the fun of almost nearly
seeing noises, sometimes clearly,
hearing shapes, accounting yearly
for this joyous quest.

So, climbing, crawling, flying through,
I beckon with a grin
and gently give my hand to you
when odd-shaped threshold comes in view,
complex sometimes, but simple too.
It's quite warm, when you're in!

Shortbread Thankyou 1989/12/27

I've tried to shorten 'bread' to 'bad'
and all the crumbs to scatter
in trying to thin the shortbread down,
but end up getting fatter.

And here's another baking triumph –
Vida's fruity turn-out
and, as my Dad so oft pronounced,
"The tea's too wet without."
The heart of Christmas is the Tum,
these munching gifts do prove,
a packed-out shrine of flavour
where there's no room to move!

But when I do sit down, reflect,
That was the 'berry' season –
when I blew merry tune on bog
and lost my nuts and reason."

Standing Joke 1993/11/03

The arse is out my trousers,
my sandal's lost its sole.
The motor car needs four new tyres,
my woolly's got a hole.
So I'll just sit here smiling
and wait for life to mend.
I can't drive out, or strut about.
Can't go past gate while in this state
and if a pound lay on the ground
I couldn't even bend.

Tartan *[Written at Inverkeithing, Scotland, during the filming of Scotch Myths]*

I came frae the Hielands tae Embro toon
an' got awfie low wi' nae friends bein' aroon'
so one night when even the moon looked sad,
I lurched out a-drinkin' an' got very bad.

I don't really know how I got tae ma bed
wi' a spinnin', careerin' an' nauseous head,
but one thing fur certain, I'd have tae think quick
of somethin' engagin' tae stop bein' sick.

So I stared at the curtain which moved up an' doon
splashed wi' tar frae the windie an' lit by the moon,
but nae matter whit squintin' an' focus I tried,
that windie-frame pattern just spread side tae side.

So with this perception, I leapt up tae shout,
"It's tartan, it's tartan!" an' then I passed out.
But you out there, don't think I've been clever –
I'm probably stuck wi' the pattern furever.

Ron as 'The Bonny Hielan' Laddie' in Scotch Myths (dir. Murray Grigor) for Channel 4 TV, 1982/07

10p Travel Fare late 1975

Our friend Teresa, girl of go,
played some games with sister Jo
in the back of parents' car
on Scottish holiday, afar.

Returning home 'cross Forth of Firth
they conjured tricks and made much mirth
so, seeing her talent to amuse,
Teresa thought she'd get her dues.

Teresa sees a bright 10p
and can't get it to stay on knee
but, being this new conjurer's girl
caught up in showbiz starry whirl,
she says, "I'll make it vanish fast!"
and holds it in her teeth at last.

A gasp! A cough! A spluttered noise,
and suddenly she's lost her poise
for coin has tipped upon the brink
and dropped down into – where'd you think?

Her stomach, working on digestion,
got a shock and asked a question,
"Gawd, Your Majesty, what now?
I plainly see your furrowed brow,
but look, I must keep food ongoing –
fate? – there is no way of knowing –
but you might be no more use
stained by my digestive juice.
Pray, just rest there, 10p new,
and I will try to work round you,
then, when solids come (like stew),
we'll see if they can force you through."

"Great Crusted Crown's of Empire's Fight!
Please do not whisper of my plight,
for if my subjects do get told,
I and my kingdom will be sold!
Instead, do muster all your strength
to get me journeying at length
towards the final exit proud –
and hope the guns are not too loud!"

Now, back to inside toil and strife
with X-rays, proddings – soon the knife?
"No, but take some figs my lass
and Queenie surely through will pass.
If not, we'll have to dig to seize'er
using blades and tweaky tweezer."

On 3rd September '75
Teresa's 10p took its dive.
By 23rd, there was no motion
(none that would bring joy-emotion).

Deep inside, to cheat the knife,
stomach strained for its dear life
and got this coin of realm engaged
in twisty passage, fair enraged
by rough milled edge that scraped its side,
so passage pushed – Oh, how it cried! –
and Madam Highness deeply moved
to firing-chamber, oiled and grooved.

On 24th, our friend Teresa
sat on throne and did a beeza –
bothered not to check its weight
cos of boring three weeks wait.

Sister Jo was next on throne
and noticed something black – A stone? –
Oh, no! It was not that she'd seen –
it was our black-faced negro Queen
a-lying there in not much state
but soon fished out to glare at fate
of being mounted on a plaque.
She screams, "I'm really white, not black!"

So, if you swallow coins, make sure
you've got a beeza aperture.

The Pear-Shaped Man 1973

The pear-shaped man with watery eyes
has large fat-stained waistcoat confining his sighs,
has notepads of eyelids that register lies
and curly hat, never chat, wobbly thighs.

The Pen 1969

There's more to this than meets the pen.
Surely I could . . ? But then,
the brain does clog from time to time
so I shall search another line
of outlets for these mad ideas,
perhaps a tapdance? That's for ears
that cannot see the shoes that gleam
and leap about in fervent steam.
"Expressivo Analyses??!"
No, a gentle breeze
that blows the brain and clears the shit.
"Now then, now then!" That does fit.
There's *still* more here to meet the pen.
Surely I could . . ? "Not again!"

From a 1966 notebook

The Well-Appointed Roll 1986/12/14

A toilet-roll is oft ill-placed,
seldom reached from where you're faced.
So, I'm moved to observation –
something vital to our nation:
twisting round while on the throne
is *the* main cause of back-twinge moan.

The next daft action we must count
is which way round the roll we mount.

Some put the paper tail behind
so it rolls down just like a blind,
except there's seldom found a cord
to pull, allowing you to find
the end essential to your need –
a soothing segment, ending deed.

It's true, the man before could fix
a cord-pull, hardly taking up two ticks
but, after his evacuation,
he's shot out with loud elation,
leaving next to pick and fumble,
losing temper – flaming grumble.

No, the roll must be turned round
so soothing segment can be found,
relieving paper constipation
and the grumbles of our nation.

To A New Couple 1992/07/10

When in doubt,
fight it out.
        When in love,
        wear a glove.
                When in bath,
                have a laugh.
                      When on moon,
                      you've gone too soon!

To Sam Smith late 1970s

[Sam Smith (1908-1983) was an innovative, very English woodcarver/ painter, now oft copied and seldom acknowledged. His quasi-trademark was GENUINE ENGLAND.]

Oh Sam, Dear Sam, I wished you lived nearer
then I could come visit to get matters clearer
like problems of clothing in fashion-clad land,
loud Fission of Fusion, the splashing-mad band! –

Ah, let me pause here, explaining this notion
that I'm in Autumnal Confusion of Motion!

See, you've seen through people with shoes on their ears
and wetted your washes with artistic tears
and I've still to do it – well, maybe I've tied lace
to stumble through stubble to face up to up-face.
So I'll just remind you of something I've said:
"If feet can't go walking, proceed on your head."
Oh Sam, Dear Sam, and warm smily Glad,
Eyes see youse,
        Well be youse,
                From Ron, the sound lad.

A Sam Smith drawing for his own 'Illistated' version of 'Fallables', presented to Ron

Two Bottles Bordeaux Thankyou 1991/01/17

Bordeaux! Bordeaux! To cause a glow!
Sang de la terre! Mon Dieu! Ho! Ho!
My '75s are coming good
so your two '86s should
lay down to rest, with your name on,
maturing gently, pleasing Ron,
then, when drinking time falls due,
I'll know the pleasure came from you.

Maybe then with glass I'll rest,
with antique book on wisdom quest
and stop going daft at table-tennis,
chucking bat with awful menace,
swearing, leaping in the air,
grumping, growling like a bear
that's stuck its tongue in acid-beaker –
over-eager honey-seeker.

A wave to you, and wrinkled grin.
It's only modern life we're in!

Two Fellows pre 1974 *Fallables p.87*

Come sit beside me on a wall,
(really I'm not here at all)
examine pavement, shuffle boot,
feel in pocket – off you shoot.
To where indeed with glasses dark
cos twilight's here so 'What a lark!'

"A lark!" I said, and someone frowned,
a flush-faced man who made no sound
save that of ears along the ground,
that home-made lump of beery mound.
He's drunk his tears, peed out again,
cried out inside like other men
and now, in realising life,
he's off to belt his home's neat wife.

Unbuilding pre 1974   *Fallables p.93*

A crumbled wall, a crumbled head,
a gritty tooth to chew.
"Unbuild, unbuild" the council say,
but what are they to *you*!
But you *will* chew and maybe eat
those bricks that fall about your feet,
excreting them in rows and rows,
called 'houses' that do scare the crows,
so they all sit in yonder tree
and 'Caw, caw, caw' at you and me.

So we'll get head down, plodding on
through thick and thicker, spirit gone,
trying more with less to guess
the size of deep dug pitty mess
in which we'll splosh, not caring less.
But those of us with plug in socket
will have a ladder stowed in pocket –
to climb out with.

Valentines 2007   *[Written in response to a BBC Radio3 competition in 2007 for*
                          new 'Valentine' messages –of course I never got a reply.]

1. I'm glad we've got an understanding,
honey pie, my leg of lamb,
that there'll be no more philand'ring
after diverse kinds of ham.

                                          (alt.)
For our spaceship's exploration,   We shouldn't need now to explore,
pretty pheasant, sacred cow;   my pleasant pheasant, leaping deer.
for our fond anticipation   It's only you that I adore
let's go make a sandwich now.   so let's just make a sandwich here.

2. Tulips and daffodils, robins and tits
push through or twitter or swing on their bits.
Pheasants are squawking and need a good oil.
Gardeners start to plant seeds in the soil.

A boy with a stick whips off daffodil heads
and pigeons have dug up the gardener's beds.
Pheasants are flat: crossed the road far too late.
Know what I mean, Gal? I think we should mate.

read right

Alcoholic Intake pre 1974 *Fallables p.10*

Is the speed that people sip/guzzle beer or other intoxicating liquor and therefore the speed they get pissed directly proportional to their desire/need to press on in their resolving of life's problems? – which could mean a nice early death!

Another Night Thought 1973 *Fallables p.51*

The jangling, chipped mobile that is my window of vision makes thought very tiring.

Should I bother at all?

The little onward-beating heart of my son bashes on through the night, its strong signal being transmitted through and across several layers of pillows.
   "It's half-past-bleedin'-four of a mid-cold September morning and the loudest thing for miles around is the scratching of beard and conformist HB pencil!"
   Agitated sticky legs in bed clothing slide slowly up, the body's only answer to another removed part of itself having flashed the bedside illumination department into positive mode.
   The counterpointed duet of miniature heavy breathing and onward-bashing life-pump forever continues beside me in defiance of the social laws of 1973 and reminds me how innocently fresh is young life, to be soon stained and bleached in alternating frenzy before it even has time to realise just how freshly innocent it is.
   I blink my eyes for some inkling of orientation, but the high-pitched multi-signals whine and cascade about in my head just to make things quite clear that they're not going to be harassed into full-powered service tonight. I really must design a multi-signal-scrambling-decoder for trapping these essential little fly buggers – except that I don't have the technical knowledge and I'd certainly burst at least one ear drum trying to fit it in!

All of life is bits and pieces.
Pieces and bits is life of all.
"Palindrome!" I hear you call,
outspoken figure of spoken wall,
outlasted head of buzzy bee?

And what does all this mean to *me*?
It means my son *will* fit in place
and fetch his boots to run the race.
Mind you, the boots are on wrong feet
which makes us smile – cross-leggèd feat!

The human module multiplies.
"Empty the seas and fill the skies!"
He who sees has not got eyes,
he who breathes broadcasts his lies –
and on and on – perpetuate.
I'm going to sleep, it's far too late!

Beer Posture pre 1974 *Fallables p.9*

In tight-formed jostling company, if one holds one's beer mug with straight arm downwards, one may get it rapped round one's balls, or the contents out of control down one's trousers. If it's up near the mouth. it may get burst on chin or teeth. Therefore it must be held with elbow at right angles and the mug cuddled in near the navel.

Below Bungalow pre 1970 *Fallables p.37*

One fine and gloomy night, while taking my body for a walk past many soothingly whispery hedgerow growths, my eyes noticed a bungalow porch light which dictated the policy of activity in its immediate region. Dizzily entranced by the yellow novelty, I floated free as wood smoke and fluttered around the noisy house, while my anaesthetised feet padded cement steps up to the front door.
   The brass key was there, at shoulder height.
   Assaulted by a tumbler of wine and the smell of much mixed nervous human activity, I was soon crawling about on several elbows, being splashed from high above by excess wine while my eyes, ears and mouth were up there and at the same level of height of depth as everyone else, adding to the massed attempt to obliterate the loud dancing-music which obliterated the loud dancing which packed the conversations into pouring constipations.
   Straining to ascend off the shattered glass cigarette floor in earnest attempt to join my head apertures and their height of depth sound bouncings, I had failed to allow for their wine intake and just glimpsed them rushing past in their plunge to a new yesterday. Realising that I was now unrepresented in the 5 ft 11 inch society, I searched my soul, but had become insufficiently double-jointed to see round the back!

Finding myself in the coal bunker at the back of the bungalow I did nothing till the morning of dawning when maximum light was to be utilised for a rather essential cold water wash under an outside tap, and I was soon back on the solid road remarking that the hedgerows' newborn leaves utter great things.

Bifurcated – Half Truncated pre 1970 *Fallables p.96*

I was caused to go for a walk, to get some fresh m-m-m-m-m-m-m-

The socks in my shoes would not move together. They were chosen from the same drawer but were not a pair!

Two different frictions made the soles of my life grate upon the uppers of my loaf.

Gravel crunched and a large coniferous variety of evergreen-layered tree waved the path forward as clear.

And discs of stereophonic coverage permeated the accompanying orchestra's instruments and the reshaped discs spun off slowly, but in great number, from the heads of the mouths that fed the instruments.But vinyl discs don't spin at the same wave as evergreen-layered branches and an almighty crash occurred soon after.

The news had not reached the papers of news by the next day and thirteen days later came out as:

   '683 valuable discs broken by irresponsible
    youth in coma-like disturbity'.

Blessing Of Art Craft pre 1974 *Fallables p.65*

Now that this good party of concerted artistes is safely ensconced in the vessel that is to be its forward conducting medium, let all good-thinking people wish it the Speed of God and safe from the influence of diverse foreign bodies that lurk in animated suspension in this murky putrescence of Thames.

Forever Onward through contraceptive devices and old sticks, carrying the good words to new and freshly rotting society, signalling the path of Entertaining Effervescence and weaving artistic patterns of dirty foam while endeavouring to avoid and repel all hellish floating things that do seek to sink its buoyant ideals.

Brain Slivers pre 1970   *Fallables p.13*

If the makeup of the whole of a person's being was represented by a frozen block of egg yolks and whites (colour coded – dyed different colours) then any other person wishing to investigate and make conscious or broadcast his feelings upon this being might have to take a sample or sliver through the block or might collect a number of such slivers, some from other people's different angle scanning of that being, then I would suggest that the picture of flat slivers built up would in no way give the many complex proportions of shapes originally in the block. In fact, some people's remembering of the exact colours and their proportions might be so far out as to scramble the possible building of any picture.
   How does a biographer give his idea of a true picture of a person?
   If he discounts other people's slivers, he can give only his limited view, and the true proportions of the 3-dimensional many coloured 'whites' and yolks may be grossly misrepresented. If he includes other people's slivers, he may well perpetuate damaging myths about that person.

Circular Frustration pre 1970   *Fallables p.27*

A man sits alone on a bus seat, desperate for the comfort of someone, or even a young female semi-innocent, to sit beside him, but trying so hard to look like he's not caring and actually scaring everyone off.

Conceived pre 1974   *Fallables p.90*

My casual posture, feet crossed and resting 3 ft (914.5 mm) high up the door frame of the train carriage, my wry chuckling as I conceive notions for this wee book, certainly have had an effect on the middle-aged Polish man and his Welsh wife who sit opposite each other at the window. She's got her stocking feet right up between his legs and cuddles his feet in her ample bosom, having previously removed his shoes and socks and displayed them in sideways V-sign on the little shelf at the window.
   The couple exhibit great joy of life.
   Maybe they've got me going and not me them since I'm so used to seeing dribbly noddings on trains.

Environment pre 1974 *Fallables p.77*

Three pieces of large crumpled brown paper,
twitching and dying,
a rusty iron-bed-springs frame
and a little boy,
aged 7
with fair hair –
and rocks to throw at passing public transport!

Exclamation Sideways pre 1974 *Fallables p.94*

My eyes are dim – up to the brim.
I lurk in shadows and them in me.

My eyes are green – to go unseen.
I sneak about through greenereee.

My eyes are blue to see through *you*.
"Who, me? – No, never! – Who said that?"
It's you! "It's *who*?" Him, over there,
that one with face beneath his hair
and if you stand like that and stare
he'll very soon return to lair
and gather strength from close walls there
and preen his length, and balls, and hair,
emerging again in a fresh pair of trousers and lighter weight shoes
to take the weight off his soul.

"Forever Onward!" shouted me, and the man at the bus-stop went spinning round and round trying to reach the correct change in his left-side back pocket with his right hand. God stopped all that of course by sneaking a hurriedly hand-written clause into the back of everyone's bible in the middle of the night with a silver threepenny bit under everyone's pillow.

And a fat greasy lady fell to a dead position out of a flat storey while attempting to see just how one of the TV newsreaders did his hair at the back.

Life continued, and the rubbed and burst blisters were incorporated in the universal art of melting the ice-blocks in which the Governmental Bleeders preserved everything that had been preserved.

"When, and by whom??"

It is not prepared to answer its predicament or disclose its recent whereabouts. However, it will say that everything is being done to see that whatever attempts that are made on the whereabouts of its disclosures will be judged by their predicament and a positive answer will be prepared.

Expert Docking In Newcastle 1990

[names have been changed to protect the author]

"He will be one surprised little pixie!" – were the words reported to have been pitched by Dr. D. V. Kakkar's secretary when a bill covering a substantial amount of work was presented by three Northern musician/composers.

General Practitioner Kakkar was a very wealthy Indian gentleman "connected to" several large businesses including a chain of Rest Homes, all run from the Channel Islands. The musicians, Bolder, Adamson and Mathieson ("B.A.M." in my files) were all working extensively in live rock and jazz in the North-East. Adamson spearheaded their extra knowledge of computers and electronics.

Sometime in 1989, Kakkar decided to make a feature film, and to dance in it. He had practised neither of these arts before. Through a 'helper', he contacted Bolder to start composing some tests/demos towards the film music and dance sequences. None of the three had much experience of this specialist area.

I suppose that the excitement of working in a new discipline with its potentially larger catchment area, and knowing that the backer was rich, led our trio to perform naive acts of exuberance without question. And no doubt Kakkar had seldom encountered such willing participation in his other 'operations'.

Was the situation ready for a Jimmy Knapp (former Scottish trade union leader) who would have, "shat here on mu shootcaishe ti shecure a shucksheshful shettlement – furever, if neshesharry"? There was no "shitting" on anything – the boys were up, sometimes half the night, and running all their gear to steaming heat making computer sequences and multitrack tapes in the then rock/pop idiom. The normal trade 'demo' wall was soon scaled and they were off across hill and dale, leaping and frolicking, altering voicings and rhythms as instructed by Kakkar and his boys. Bolder's girlfriend and professional singer Daisy Wheeler was the main voice, for a short time, before Kakkar preferred the quasi-Michael Jackson quiver of his man, Chas Chortle.

So, B.A.M. were composing songs and dance sequences, all to a high standard demo stage in their home studio, the 8-track tapes from which could have been 'beefed' in a bigger studio to have served the final purpose adequately. Contracts? Kakkar was not going to commit himself, not with all that material so freely served on a hot plate. And the composers imagined they'd found a rich patron – at last!

But the subject of money was going to get raised sometime. Three months into the job, around April 1990, Bolder went to the Musicians' Union North-East representative to get some advice on rates. The ensuing bill, calculated as normal for recording sessions and adding up to an awful lot, raised that secretary's voice a few tones.

The short of it is that the M.U. resolved to back B.A.M and Wheeler to see Kakkar in Court. So the Great Engine of the Law puffed, whined and ground into forward movement – well, some of it was forward.

Our boys were working with the New Tools: the "Schlipp Rule and the Schpanner" (Gerard Hoffnung). It's always been difficult and probably futile to describe the intricacies of music, especially in a Court of Law, but just add the many existing preconceptions to the further invisible, often incomprehensible, hyper-whir of oxide particles and digits.Call for an Expert!

I had not been able to join the M.U. for many years since I was keeping my head well down in the undergrowth, building and operating a nest with every conceivable fibre of new technology, and breaking every rule that has ever been imagined. But actually I am concerned only with the feelings of passion and fun and their projection as dialogue into society for a reasonable return. It was this experience that made me a so-called Expert.

Later, I was to make hours of music for Central TV maths and science series and got to know the Chairman of the M.U. quite well. He recommended me for this case.

Backed by the impeccably implacable experience of Newcastle solicitor Roderick Hard-Taxman, I began in the normal way by reading all documentation and listening to the tapes. It was obvious to me that the compositions were clearly laid out although not very inspiring – as MOR rock – and would have given any Media executive ample opportunity to comment or discontinue negotiations at first demo stage. But Kakkar asked both for certain pieces to be developed or re-worked and for new pieces, denying all this later. And wait till you hear about the film!

I made a thorough analysis of all material and scrutinised the computer-sequencer charts for comparison. B.A.M. were working by the generally-accepted method in this field: a sequence, usually of rhythm patterns, bass, chords and fills for subsequent triggering of any choice of synthesized and sampled sounds, is built in the computer sequencer and either run in synchronization with a multitrack tape by means of a "SMPTE" control track or, simply, the triggered sounds are transferred to some tracks on the tape, to which live-performed instruments and voices are added.

But it's not appropriate to charge full recording session rates. In this complete 'making' of music, time is spent in computer-fiddling, talking, writing, experimenting and performing. When I co-ordinated and wrote the booklet "Commissioning Guidelines For The Electro-Composer" (pub. Association of Professional Composers), the research panel came to the conclusion that it was more sensible to charge either a rate per hour of working time or a rate per minute of finished music, both reconciled by our finding that, over a prolonged stretch of time, say one month, about one minute can be composed, performed and finished in one day, with all the obvious fluctuations of varying density.

So I had to suggest reduction of the M.U.-based claim by at least half, still leaving a considerable sum. My first report was loaded with plenty of "based on a reasonably ideal working relationship between film maker and composer" and you've already worked out that B.A.M.'s willingness to proceed was inversely proportional to Kakkar's ability to decide what he wanted.

In response, Kakkar's expert's report arrived a year later. In his obvious striving to rubbish B.A.M.'s work, he fell over! There was an all-too-repetitive bleat of "not expected of first-class composers of film music" and a glaring error of mistaking computer floppy-disc charts for 24-track tape sheets. The clues were that there was a box in the top-left corner called "Disc Title" and no mention of the live-performed sounds like "voices", "guitar" or "saxophone". Actually I missed one but, adrenalized later in the Witness Box, I spotted a box for "MIDI Channel" – producing a stern glare at Kakkar from his barrister.

Ah, to the Witness Box – even hotter than the steaming glass lifts sliding up and down the outside of the multi-million pound Newcastle Crown Court. The architect had not noticed that the sun's arc would enable perfect cooking of the lifts' contents: maybe the design was done in November or there was intent to get Court participants up to temperature.

In Court, I sat behind the link-men of the drama. Our side had a sharp little beady-eyed barrister, fresh from London, opposed by a North-Eastern hulk with a very torn gown (apparently a ploy to be "a man of the people"). Frequently did he push down on the broad and expensive light-oak table – and, with every creak and groan, our little fellow went up in the air. For three days I sat there, passing the odd bit of paper to our man with, "Try him on tempo"(to do with designing dance sequences) or "That's impossible because ...".

Proceedings were enlivened by an early recital of B.A.M.'s work, suitably ricochetting round the cream plaster. "Well, at least we know it's not Beethoven!" smirked the Honourable Judge. "That's not the original tape!" cried the Defendents. But it was – and their auditioning machine must have been not so much a Ghetto Blaster as a Gecko Blister.

A section of the finished film, transferred to video, was next. Apparently shot in and around Newcastle, with a bit of Buckingham Palace, it concerned the arrival and protection of the "*King of Kantipur*". Two characters are on screen, both facing the camera. One turns his eyes (only) to the other and, with a pause surpassing even the best Dawn French, the henchman is prompted to ask, "Have – you – got – the – gun – boss?" Another scene prophetically has our hero having the change shaken from his pockets, but the best bit was the dancing – you know that kind of jumping you do to shake down your rumpled trouser legs, all to that most niggly-wiggly Indian film music. (Send for the great bamboo flute of Hari Prasad Chaurasia, for Gawd's sake!). Muffled mirth spluttered across the Courtroom floor. Listen, the boys were well out of this one.

At another point, the Judge went off on some interrogative spur with, "I am minded to suggest that Mr. Adamson be dispatched forthwith by aer-io-plane to the Isle of Wight to attempt retrieval of the aforementioned diary." All the while, from day to day, Dr. Kakkar came and went, treating the Court "as a convenience".

Undergoing cross-examination in the Witness Box is a gruelling and often upsetting experience. Lewis Carroll's got nothing on this. The rule is, "Counsel" (interrogating barrister) can ask any leading or loaded question, no matter how unfair it may seem, and you cannot retort – only if you can make the Judge smile – without stretching to Oscar Wilde-ness. It turned out that Kakkar's man was a criminal specialist and had particularly aggressive and sneering manners – also some ploys that would have raised a glass, right into his face, in any friendly meeting-house.

It took me about an hour to get up to speed, during which time I completely forgot how I had arrived at a particular rate per day. Then I was stabbed with a question about the Defendants' accusation of B.A.M.'s plagiarizing of the "High Chaparral" theme (which turned out to be "The Magnificent Seven" anyway!) "Mr. Geesin, I don't suppose you've even checked this music since you 'don't listen to that sort of thing'?" (True. I prefer Coleman Hawkins, Earl Hines, Elgar, Varèse & Berio.) Taking a calculated risk, I leant forward with a mouth like I was spitting lemon pips and retorted, "My Dear Fellow …', drawing instant admonishment and a light smirk from the Judge. After apologizing, I continued, "As a matter of fact, I looked in the Radio Times and, there, that very day, was the said programme. I recorded it off the television to examine it thoroughly. In fact, as a professional composer and musicologist, I can find any piece of music in the world!" But was glad not to be challenged on that one. His worst ploy was to keep saying, "I'm sorry?" to a perfectly well-articulated reply. When I rumbled this, I leant forward (again) and presented a closed mouth and raised eyebrows, the silent questioning riposte being, "And so am I! Your move!", forcing him to repeat what I'd replied in the first place. Oh yes, I'm an avid student of Mr. Gamesmanship, Stephen Potter.

Then, just as Kakkar was going to be razor-bladed by our man, it was Friday and we all had to go home. My reports were in and work done, but I was sad to miss the second session where Kakkar was "left substantially discredited". Nice pun too. The Judge "preferred the Plaintiff's (B.A.M. & Wheeler) account of events to that of Dr. Kakkar", found in the Plaintiff's favour and not unreasonably knocked my suggested rate of £500/day down to £375/day, adding substantial interest. He also awarded Wheeler her full claim for session fees and ordered Dr. Kakkar to pay the Plaintiff's full costs.

If you're going to be a Professional Witness, you'll need deep breathing, a sense of humour, a bit of knowledge and at least a pint of beer at lunchtime. If you're a musician/composer, get contracted. Two bits of paper might save four years, and six days in Court.

Soon after, the "surprised little pixie" was persuaded to trundle his bag of gold over the edge of his high toadstool.

Friend Relations pre 1974   *Fallables p.38*

If one tries to 'find' oneself in one's friends, there will constantly be a state of tension in those relationships. If one 'finds' oneself in one's work or life-endeavours, the result can be shared with one's friends and all will be well.

Of course if one 'finds' oneself correctly, but certain friends do not, and they try to find themselves through one, or even through one's findings, all will not be well!

All this supposes that the persons mentioned want to go on the search trek in the first place.

Heat pre 1974   *Fallables p.89*

Hot late Summer day
train carriage glass box
lady's jacket off
window open
sweaty sigh.

Nobody's noticed the heater switches!

I Dream Of Life pre 1974   *Fallables p.78*

Our 4 month old baby, naked to the air and grass of the world, lies side by side in a perfect row with his 5 naked sextuplet brothers – all kicking in slow motion like upturned tortoises. Our square red-brick house stands some 100 yards away (as I look into the Sun) with its french windows open. My father and mother stand nearer to the babies than I and the whole ensemble is posed on an interminable expanse of medium-cut grass.

My father gently picks up the nearest little one and begins to fit its harness on. This harness is of special metal and encases the head, the nuclear warhead being tightly lodged in the maximum area of wide open mouth. These babies are to be the first of a new kind of missile, powered by life. My father strokes the little soft pink downy body and exclaims how perfect a little machine it is and ideally suited for its mission.

"So," I said, "when it gets to the target area it drops the warhead and returns to our warm outstretched arms?"

"Oh no, it goes down all the way and sacrifices itself. That's why you people today are encouraged to cause multi-births. Look at the drugs that are available, and the superb advertising!"

I could not see my mother since she had got herself well hidden behind my father so I rushed to the house, through the open french windows, saw my wife sideways on to me gazing at a blank wall and screamed, "See what's happening – our baby to be plastered over half of some alien landscape! We've got to stop it!"

She turned.

"Nothing – can – be – done."

She turned away to light another cigarette.

Ideas In Trees pre 1974 *Fallables p.63*

Is a human being and his idea-thinking process like a healthy tree in that there is the stable main trunk with subsidiary branches that grow slowly and are added to through the years?

Also, with healthy deciduous trees, the leaves all come with great show every Spring and die off in the Autumn – but more come each successive year cos the tree has grown a bit so the foliage is thicker, more complex in structure – until it dies of course.

Seeds are projected from the tree and only a few are actually germinated to continue that species. Animals eat the seeds and convert them to other energies.

Then there is the decay of the tree which sometimes holds on to a little bit of life well past when it should die completely.

Mit Klappmesser (With Penknife): Ron's wood sculpture, Friedrichshöhe, Germany, 1995/07/09

In A German Forest 1995/07/09

Trees drink from the skin.
Seeds drink from the moss.
Fir cones explode.
Artists look for plastic.
Trees stand.
Sun moves.
Grass waves.
Artists think.

106 flies tickle me.
601 trees baffle me.
16 artists amuse me.
I know I exist.
I struggle up a cart track
into the forest of broken wood.
I find a man whittling.
It is me.

VERWANDLUNG: Musik und Klänge, erzeugt durch das Berühren von Schiefer, Holz und die Resonanz von Eimern. Eins der Objekte des Friedrichshöher Symposiums „Kunst auf der Höhe". TA-Fotos (2): O. ITTERSHAGEN

Ron with his 'Schieferonphon' (Slate Xylophone),
Friedrichshöhe, Germany, 1995/07/09

In Group Dressing Room 1970 *Fallables p.72*

What does one do with an old piece of linoleum, especially one that covers another old piece of linoleum. Cold on the feet and damaging on the eyeball. Frayed edges, broken by a very below average human finger, nearly fit round corners of chipped cream-painted cream furniture. Flattened, frayed cigarette stubs, carefully arranged by the little men who live under the linoleum, dance about partnered by well chosen old sticks of match. The tune is forever guitar on the guitar. A cymbal splashes to the tune of a brandished stick of drum and runs about the auditorium, bashing its head on the available hard surfaces, fastly chased by a bass note from another kind of guitar-mad guitar. The cymbal is indestructible, except by nearly-silence which skulks in a corner unable to really move or communicate with other potential nearly-silences.

Nothing more moves.

Initiation c. 1990

In 1960, although I had to have fashionable tight trousers and sideburns (improved with a 6B pencil), I had recently got a banjo and joined a very amateur local Mahogany Wardrope and his Pinetop Jazzband*. Paul Wardrope's mum had the gift of gossip and went about frowning gracefully on the little polite village of Bothwell, Lanarkshire, which in turn frowned disapprovingly on the river Clyde, about 10 miles outside Glasgow. It was her image that gave me a key description later of a person "with lipstick half way up her nose, which made a great deal of mouth".

Anyway, one of our early gigs, inevitably on a Saturday night, was in a church hall or some kind of associated club in a most sociably unsuitable area of South East Glasgow. After a typically sweaty first set, and swathed in diverse aromas from tightly-clad and rotting minds and bodies, I went for a pee. Minding my own business alone at the stained porcelain, a darkness came upon me. It was a really professional Teddyboy, nothing fancy, just the right black and white gear and a piece of granite fallen off one of Glasgow's buildings for a head.

"Nyer't'f'k'n gloor shgrrr wan kl'f'k'n oor naw f'k'n herrr!"

I frowned.

Out came, "Grrawflechni f'k'n burrrit!" and a small apparatus from his left-hand jacket pocket."

That's a complicated arrangement of finger rings", I thought. "Can't be gold." So I asked.

"Haw f'k'n erg ti f'k'n yewurr tawly heid."

Honestly, the message was not transmitting too well as he eased this mechanical aid onto his flexing right hand fingers.

A third person appeared at the toilet door. It was Mrs. Wardrope's only clarinettist son, a great deal more versed in South East Glasgow mouthery than I was or could ever hope to be.

It turned out I was being mistaken as a member of a rival Teddyboy gang and about to be knuckledusted, in brass, right through the toilet window.

It was a great deal of the right sort of mouth from Paul Wardrope that saved me.

This encouraged me to develop survival ploys of astuteness and clowning, on and off stages.

It was the drummer in this band (Jim Mullen, I think) who shouted the famous line on one of those Saturday nights, "The next dance will be a fight!"

Ron as Bonny Prince Charlie crossed with Liberace at Fingal's Cave in Scotch Myths (dir. Murray Grigor) for Channel 4 TV, 1982/07

Knock Down – Stand Up pre 1970   *Fallables p.18*

A brick came through my head.
It was projected by a thin young student at a concert where I was trying to do my performance, and it reminded me of my intentional projection of wrong words at the English Teacher when I was at school.
This time it was I who disintegrated.
The next day, some well-planted flowers and a nippy little spider that jumped quite considerable chasms to get where it wanted to go showed me that juice was still to be had for Life and, quite soon after, I found bits of myself on a train looking out at the curious modern mixture of silver birch trees growing on slag heaps. The wind, being drawn in through the open window, lifted the fibrous material on the top of my head so the Sun could heal the brick-shaped gash.
I had now gained sufficient confidence to look around.
Nobody smiled much – or even at all. Life just had to be raced and there really was no way of climbing through the lavatory window to get out of it.
Then a man with more than a few hairy £10 notes sticking out of his ears said, "We'll build a factory there, and another one over the hill there. The first one is to manufacture the people to buy the moderately priced poison that's brewed in the second one. The money gained makes my wife an old withered bag in next to no time and then I can go out and have a special house built with ceilings made entirely out of succulent young ladies' pendant breasts."
He soon achieved all this, but due to an error in carpet thickness calculation, he had to climb a ladder every day for his carnal dinner which meant that when he actually made it up to the nipple-ceiling he ate much more than originally intended. This necessitated a step up in production in the people-factory which escalated through the whole system until his bath sponge ate him.
I remain continually on the look-out for unusual behaviour from inanimate objects.

Litter Dropping pre 1970   *Fallables p.20*

I always thought the dropping of litter showed a lack of environmental relationship awareness, but could it also be linked with the 'defacing' thing in that cities, streets with paving-slabs etc. are sensed by the human as too perfect and devoid of texturous imperfections that make up the multi-levelled human life experience?
Dropping litter might also be linked with the kind of ceremonial spitting and pee-ing that is a demonstration of claim of territory (old men sitting on bench at village square or park etc. seem to spit a lot / the marvellous wide-astride attitude of the countryside pee-er claiming that bit of ground as his for that glorious moment – I am aware it's different for ladies, but maybe the same mentally, given that fright of discovery be removed!).

Living Too Close pre 1970   *Fallables p.24*

Living too close to things blunts the nose.
Living too far away from things:
    a) doesn't do anything at all,
    b) extends the nose so much that it sags and closes down,
    c) allows the nose to examine other things which are too close and therefore blunt it again.
Living at just the right distance from things is impossible cos one has to move in order to know where one is – the principle of two or more radar points plotting the position of an object.

Machines 1971   *Fallables p.33*

The motivation for too many people's lives at this time seems to be the achievement of navigating through the spikes of complex material gadgetry which has been invented as a supposed aid to living.

If a particular human is capable of handling the proper aspects of a gadget, which must include mental knowledge of its place in the Machine of Evolution, then it is possible to use it as an aid, but as there are increasing numbers of gadgets being invented and marketed, so the human brain has no time and space to see these in relation to its own life/ thought scale because, upon being born, the human is thrown immediately into a multi-armed and legged wrestling match with levers, wires, buttons and switches and fails to grasp the meaning of it all, being occupied totally in rushing to partially master the use of one before the marketeers rush in faster with ten new gleaming diversions.

March Of Time pre 1974   *Fallables p.92*

Red Brick Armies sweep past –
    window buttons tarnished –
        TV aerials at half mast –
            arms of prams certainly not shouldered –
                backyard scrap-heap haircuts growing long –
                      slate helmets askew –

smoky thought-mutterings drifting up to add to those fume-clouds of the knowledge that can only be furthered by its own mistakes.

Molecular Structure pre 1974 *Fallables p.40*

Everything is molecular structure.

Art construction in all its forms is simply the choosing of separate or possibly groups of atoms and molecules from diverse existing structures and re-grouping them with mental science.

One might start by repeating examples done by previous mental-art-scientists to get the feel of what it's about, but since each brain is complexly different from the next, so its expression has to be complexly different and one must soon press on with one's own structures – and yet there is a universal bond of molecular structure, which is another way of saying 'form/art is everywhere'.

A handbag placed on a seat becomes, visually, part of the molecular structure of that seat. If the handbag is moved to another part of that seat, the whole visual structure is changed. So, a tiny red dot placed specifically on a large white area becomes a work of art, but it's also a criticism that art is viewed too reverently since people will spend time and money to trek to view, maybe worship, the little red dot on the large white area in an art gallery but will swiftly get the handbag removed from the seat cos they want to sit down! The artist of the red dot work may have dropped the dot onto the large white area from 20 metres with an uncertain gusty wind blowing just as the handbag may have been dropped onto the seat from an overladen pair of hands.

Because I have worked for some time now on the forming of music and sounds, and through this specific endeavour have become aware of the 'molecular structure' parallel, I can see great form in 'Beautiful Landscape Traversed By Electricity Pylons', 'Tiny Aeroplane In One Expansive Sky', 'One Cup Of Tea With Spoon And Attached Shadows', 'One Bogey Slightly Protruding From Person's Nose' and, apart from when I'm blackly depressed, Life is seen from inside me to be better every day because of my positive use of the rich energy that is emitted from every thing, live or dead.

**On Emerging From A Walk-Way Tunnel
To Wait For Tube Train** pre 1974 *Fallables p.41*

Then there's this fellow sucking at the stub of a fag with three fingers pinched in, mirroring his mouth attitude. His double-buckled shoes are spanning and deeply embedded in two concrete paving slabs, showing him ready to repel all advances, metal or human.

Ladies, two, with ample flesh flapping from the bones of their legs spread themselves thickly on the tube train seat and gather in their posh polythene well-advertised shopping receptacles like a doting mother with five children.

Some people don't watch anything, in fact it has become a serious offence to acknowledge the existence of anyone else. This mode is attained by shutting down the eyelids.

I just saw a man trying not to pick his nose behind his newspaper!

Workman constantly punch each other with their mouths.

When the roaring giant of a tube train came, the fag sucker suddenly withdrew his double-buckled shoes from the concrete and became a little scuttling pixie to compete with all the other scuttling pixies, but managed a further quick change to a hunched-up half-shut-marble-eyed frowny scowling monkey as he took his tense unrest out on the floor of the tube train that was carrying him to his necessary employment.

Opening For Closing 1996/03/29

Genesis was about to release its album "Selling England By The Pound" in November 1973 and arranged a major UK tour of 14 dates for the month before. I was a friend of Peter Gabriel and he asked me to do the opening half-hour, having seen at least one of my outrageous dadaistic stream-of-subconsciousness performances. The rest of the band didn't know me. The opening night, Friday the 5th of October, was to be at the Apollo, Glasgow. For a change, I decided to do a non-entry and went out in a white technician's coat to seemingly adjust a few things and gradually move up through the gears. This was not a good idea! I managed to survive twenty minutes of the allotted half-hour, using up my best confrontational techniques of piano pounding, banjo-bashing, cymbal-slinging and screamed dialogue, but the crowd had made up its mind very early and was so incensed that fixtures and fittings were being lined up to fly. The band never went on that night. I should have known better, having been brought up, although rather politely, on the outskirts of those parts.

When I came off the stage, a mains electric fault was 'found' in the rigging, which may have been real, but I touched plenty of metalwork out there on that comparatively enormous lighting rig and got no shock! I think nerves were more frayed than wires, and none more frayed than those of Peter Gabriel, whose previous enthusing had got me on the tour in the first place. He skulked backstage, his pale face showing through his paler makeup, a sad clown indeed, with his audience of the rest of Genesis members about to turn all of him very red. Nobody, least of all me, slept much that night.

At Manchester next night I went out and hit the audience before it got me – and the rest of the tour was great – I got actual encores at two of the dates. And there was a memorable recreational rowing-boat trip with Peter Gabriel on the then bright green Sheffield canal where we philosophised the afternoon away and fished little boys' footballs out of the steaming slime. Such is the performer's lot.

Genesis went back to Glasgow at the end of the tour, without me!

Actually, I think Genesis would have preferred a safer "opener" – one who could just keep the audience ticking over while the group fine-tuned that night's Calculated Lateness Factor. *[see C.L.F. in Noun Clown]*

Indeed, when an earlier admirer, Pete Townshend, got me to open for The Who on two occasions, I went down rather too well and was subjected in the dressing-room to a little lecture from Roger Daltry who described a previous ideal opener, a female singer "of colour" who just managed to last the half-hour before being booed off.

Our Dance 1975 *Fallables p.34*

'Dance' is the cogs of bodies meshing in one section of a machine that turns out Collective Unified Expression.

Collective Unified Expression (CUE, an accident, honest!) is the cogs of small groups of life meshing in the machine that turns out Evolution Progress.

Evolution is Discovery. If we do not discover, we do not evolve. If we do not evolve, we stagnate and rot.

What is happening now, 1975 – and for some time past – is material evolvement, leaving spiritual evolvement to stagnate in the pond of Man's Over-Conscious Analysis Of His Own Deeply Natural Sub-Conscious Development (e.g., Christianity's mistaken conscious self-analysed identity). Because of this stagnation, material evolvement has grown cankerously over-dominant since materials merely serve to aid man's spiritual realisation. If the spiritual realisations become bogged in the mud of the stagnant pond, materials stagger about pulling this way and that on the lead that joins them to their master. If the master panics, the materials dash about more frenziedly and wrap the lead round themselves, tightly encircling their master too. The process of death and rot follows.

In the past, there's always been a little farmer over the hedge who jumps to the rescue – or a Hitler dressed up as a little farmer.

That which is, is and ever shall be so – despite all our efforts to analyse our destiny. But we now know a little too much for comfort and have to analyse cos we've all got some goal/task to keep us lively. I do feel we could be a bit more lively though!

Phone 1996/04/18

I am very interested in phone manner. Here is a situation. It is early Spring and I am more than reasonably shredded from creative business and social pursuits through the Winter. I need a holiday which in fact will have to be just a short break.

I phoned the travel agent and got, "Samantha – 'ow can I h-help you?" (but it sounded more like "Thamowelp?" – in the distance). I believed that the Winter stress had added deafness to my disabilities, but persevered by getting Samantha to repeat everything two or three times. Later, I humbly visited the travel agent's shrine to try a face-to-face with Samantha. The whole place could 'ear 'er, commanding the airwaves shouting her auburn hair off behind her computer in her sky-blue suit with cream cuffs trimming a recent tan. She was no beauty, but important. What she was actually doing was using the phone mouthpiece as an inefficient World War Two pilot's throat microphone: the mouthpiece was tucked away under her chin, touching her throat. The whole office, and some casual passersby could here her firm pronouncements, but the customer at the other end couldn't. Samantha had misread her 'maximisation of environment for vocational opportunity'. Instead of attempting her power-projection at three colleagues and some weary travel-trawlers, she could have used a much more varied dynamic voice-range as part of a softer seduction technique, and got all the information across, simply by speaking into the mouthpiece.

There's another kind of phone-abuse. This is when the speaker tries to see the person at the other end, by squinting down the mouthpiece. The effect is the same: an awkward attempt at importance display at one end and an annoyed or worried person at the other.

If you suspect that the incoming signal could not possibly be as weak as it sounds, take courage and humour and say, "Excuse me, but could you tell me where your phone mouthpiece is at this moment?" Usually, there is a rustling, the signal improves and you hear clearly, "Why right in front of my mouth, of course".

Poster Defacing pre 1970 *Fallables p.19*

The defacing of posters may be a natural intuitive desire to turn the perfect images thereon displayed into the imbalanced, imperfect, real-life state. Could this be true for all types of defacing? (razor-slashing other people's faces not counted!)

Railway Sleepers

[read on the John Peel BBC 'Night Ride' programme, 1968/08/14]

Railway sleepers – sleeping – their dark brown exteriors unaware of the jagged sheets of corrugated metal glaring at them. Matchbox houses look over the scene, but never really upon it. Humans from the matchbox houses have built amazing little housettes from the glaring corrugated metal – which soon corrodes and falls down. But they never quite ever fall down, but are supported by all manner of rubbish, which supports them, in a way. Humans soon follow the example as they in turn corrode and surround themselves with all manner of rubbish.

Are you corroding? Where is your little allotment with its housette all falling down? – Are you corroding?

Are your friends jagged bits of corrugated metal gradually going rusty? They're probably out building bigger erections of corrugated metal, from which will be produced many more sheets of the same – the whole adding up to a chaotic state of rust – and humans.

Reply To "Chordless Electric Drill" Newspaper Ad. Sent By Ian Breakwell From Ireland 1992/08/21

Thanking you for alerting me to what must be a revival of the Indian model, lain dormant in Ireland for some 900 years: the Chordless Effects Unit. The word is not 'Drill' but 'Dryl' (or 'Drull' in Southern India), where the strings (or cords), when they are there at all, are too far apart to form chords. This early technological mistake largely influenced the development of Monodic Modality in that southern continent and provoked the Northquesting Nomadic Mobility, maddening the Northern Nobility, that deposited the magnificently grunting Bullfydl (a huge one-string accompanying instrument made originally of burial-boxes, all too necessary for that Nomadic Trybe, with the gut of the incumbent deftly interwoven with a cow's tail and stretched across it to form the Stryng) in Romania and the Dryl in Ireland.

This really does prove the extent to which nervous Technological Twitches influenced, on a global scale, the Merry Musing Wayfarer class such that it found itself devoted to unravelling the all-too-frequent technological puzzles thrown up into society out of the metaphorical Thin Minds (and even this phrase metamorphosed to Tin Mines) by those who found it necessary to allay their itches by means of underground scratching. It was by this process that those Merry Musing Wayfarers were forced to become Artists and Creators – these very words crystallising out of their early expostulation, "*That's a far test from a crater!*" as they were confronted by having to defuse yet another Technological Time Bomb.

Return 1992/10/03

We squashed and jostled into the 757 and took off from Menorca on time at 6pm. Posh TV screens kept us minutely sprayed with height and speed data, and how many times the craft had been painted. What it didn't give us was the number of times the most-beautiful of the painted hostesses licked her fingers to transfer plastic tumblers and serviettes to our pews. Captain God explained that we would be 'cruising' for some 15mins extra due to Spanish flight routing.

Overflowing a seat opposite was a fat lady with a normal baby – but not for long! The crying subtly ascended through some kind of distortion-unit to an impersonation of Louis Armstrong's throat at double-speed. Wiping the sweat from the sides of her nose, the mother casually chatted away in Lutonese to someone adjacent who spoke the same language. Frantic dummy-poking was rejected. Position-changes merely found new airwaves.

I did note that the stewardesses' scurrying was accelerating.

Then, it came. Simultaneously with the Captain's announcement that, due to the 'slight re-routing', we would have to refuel at Nantes (on the Loire) the baby jettisoned all its fuel – over mother, father and daughter – the yellow spume somehow matched the aeroplane's fuel, and the number of times it had been painted. Significantly, the screen directly above us stepped out of line, turned up its eye and gave up its picture.

The baby, now lead singer in Puke's Chorus and driving the whole congregation daft, rasped its protest as we hit Nantes runway. I always knew the French were a nation of farmers. This runway was ploughed – and the stewardesses smiles had detached themselves to be nervously waved about on crudely-fashioned twigs.

I dare say that Nantes is as beautiful as any other place on the Loire, but we couldn't get off to confirm that, and the '20 minute' stop threatened to become as long as a French lunch.

The baby was swabbed, duty-frees finally massaged wallets into submission and we arrived at Gatwick at 10pm.

Never think you're going to have a good time everywhere!

Scraped Youth pre 1970   *Fallables p.11*

I've just travelled on a train that has had its inside scraped and engraved with the upside-down, sideways, capitals language of fanatics of the football game.

If only they could make this even a little communicative of what's careering about in their heads, maybe there would be less physical damage done.

Search Light For Quality 1987/01/–

"Rotting Hill – Shocking Hill!" was the 52 bus-conductor's cabaret turn on his every approach to Notting Hill. He could also have been describing the Notting Hill Gate Classic Cinema around 1969.

At one late-night showing, the main picture was projected in reel-order: 1, 2, 5, 4, 6, 3, 7. The line I took with the manager was that, as a composer who worked quite a lot in films, I really needed to see equal commitment all along the picture's beam to the Public. "I don't see any other dissatisfied customers!" was his illuminating reply. Actually, he could have argued sharply that his cinema was committedly continuing the fashionable creative process of picture-montage. Maybe the hyperceptive artist community of Shocking Hill recognised this extra input, or was it just stupefied with diverse substances?

This cinema had also capitalised on the psycho-acoustic phenomenon prevalent in rock music of suggesting a heightened intensity by simulating loudness-distortion with 'fuzz' – it had plainly blown its speaker cone, rendering all dialogue and music as if through comb-and-paper. Effects, like feet on gravel and door latches, inherently with a good deal of sharp crunchiness, were barely affected though.

The projectors' arc-lamps were not so much set as sun-set, through a fog. How poignantly vignetted was the ice in Alexander Nevsky – but Eisenstein would have stabbed the projectionist with icicles.

Were these modifications other super-sixties art-works? No, just the Public getting what it wanted – somewhere warm with a partially-random flicker – a soothing log fire with plenty of crackle.

A bit further back, at age 16 in 1959, I experienced another kind of self-inflicted pain – on holiday in Brodick, Isle of Arran, Clyde Estuary. On Saturday nights in the summer, the Picture House became the Dance Hall. The high splintery stage was commanded by a brown elephant of an electric gramophone roaring 78rpm hits of the period. Fronting this orchestra was a thin, moustached gentleman confined in a light-grey suit. With nothing but a pole up his back and a snare drum wedged between his legs, he brushed and bashed away with great panache like he was furiously sewing up a leaking willie with a giant needle and thread.

But, to the Picture House, haven of sexual preliminaries. Imagining that everyone else is hypnotically distracted by the flickering beam, every young person settles down to the unrestful practice of touching. Any part of the body may be used: feet may gently heel-and-toe sideways until contact is reached, too often an empty ice-cream carton; knees may be twitched over with a cough; the armrest serves either as the top of a wall for elbow-juggling or as a thick rope along which fingers may walk or slide, paralleling many antics of the little folk in big cartoons; after scratching the back of one's head, a good throat-clearance will throw one's arm round the victim with some force, except that both arm and victim tend to become numb and partially-detached; shoulders may be ground to a firm paste.

I chose the head itself, reasoning I suppose that if I got it down onto her shoulder, the very weight would transmit the intensity of my feelings. So, oblivious to the jolly fun of missile exchanges – shoes, jackets, bags, confectionary and words – all maliciously aimed to damage any possible enjoyment of The Picture by Groan-Ups, I began. At half-an-inch a minute, would she meet me half way and solder skulls? What prickle of adventure this space-journey of prowess demonstrated before the great God-Screen. Bits of loves and deaths floated past in the windows of the multiplex eye. A Himalayan avalanche of monks' voices entoned encouragement. My head inclined now at 45 degrees. She had moved, just to test if I had power enough for the crusade. I journeyed on, my skull-ship zinging with supersonic pulses, the Big Picture fuzzily sliding off its own screen – and my neck acupunctured by the odd shoe. Brylcreem kept my hair on anyway. Then I was there, landed, and orange electricity flooded the building encouraging lumpy and fleshy matter to pile over us and squirt out of it. I was in no position to flow with the tide or protect my lovely purple anemone. Later, we enjoyed a fresh tomorrow's-bread-roll out of the back of the bakery and I went back to my damp tent, near the river of course, to nurse (and exacerbate) the ache of adolescent rheumatism.

Even further back into my Scottish formative years, I describe for you the strong impression of pee-dribbled short trousers sealed with well-rubbed butter and liquorice-flavoured chewing-gum, brought to a pungent rancidity in the drenched queue of a Clyde Valley Saturday Morning Picture House Club, all wrapped up in the repercussions of early-morning beans, to suggest that you might as well sit on your own toilet with a video as go to the pictures at all.

Searching *Fallables p.22*

1961
Curses fiendish on Mankind
since to ignorance it is inclined.
It learns and learns and learns and learns
but no true knowledge does it find
since it, having lost the Art of Life,
goes instead in search of wife.

1971
A human is not a human without another human.

Self Note 1970 　　　　　　　　　　　　　　　　　　　　　　　　*Fallables p.12*

When I started travelling extensively in trains (1966), which tend to go faster than bicycle, car or bus, I could think better. Then that was changed by my weaker side of brain and I could no longer 'get inspired'.

　Now I find I'm getting 'inspired top-off-the-brain' signals and ideas while travelling in an aeroplane – at the window and looking out at the snowy cotton-wool cloud land (*no* artificial stimulants!). This helps me concentrate and drift into more intense areas of thought. I *must* be able to get this brain condition at nearly *all* times. Is it that in this society there is much too much material clutter, which is a manifestation (infestation) of the weaker sides of brains everywhere, and this is placed as a permanent distraction from, and avoidance of, truth (the complex abstractual reasoning of which we are all capable)? Are humans frightened of discovering their purpose or, rather better, non-purpose and, if this occurred, would mass suicide occur or would there be a new amazing enlightened state of humanity with everyone truly an individual and fully capable of 'switching on' everyone else?

Sharp Saddle 1984/02/07

I'm full of musical dough
that's made from lots of flower.
If I don't get my pedals to open,
I won't be able to handle bars
or really try cycling at all.
My speaking will be rusty spokes
that make a lot of noise in the wind
and keep braking.

Sound pre 1970 　　　　　　　　　　　　　　　　　　　　　　　　*Fallables p.17*

"Darling, if you put your ear close to mine, you'll hear last night's electric, whining, beating group that should still be issuing from the brain tissue."

Spider's Life 2012/06/22

A spider spins a very thin straggly web that is attached to many bits of human-made objects. It catches a very tired hoverfly and spins a subsidiary cocoon for it. Through the cocoon, it sucks the hoverfly's brains out – to get enough energy to spin a very thin straggly web.

The Poy Tree dateless!

The Poy Tree, originating in China, is related to the Litter Chewer plant, the main difference being that, whereas the latter consumes litter in the form of letters, the former synthesises itself from tomes in the earth. It is best known for its intoxicating Rye-Ming seeds.

The buds appear in late Winter and, although lacking the usual protective sticky reason, are covered in airs that interact most favourably with the wind to produce little frayed Z's of sound, so often quoted in early Spring compositions by budding composters. In fact, it is the vibratory interaction with the wind that creates sufficient warmth for the buds to develop and open.

The flowers appear in March and exhibit but two petals. These take the form of a pair of hairy tufts that twitch from time to time to attract the early B's – away from the Litter Chewer. The tree was originally named the Ploy Tree in the 16th Century due to a similarity of its tuft-twitching to the movement of scientists' and intellectuals' eyebrows when their owners wished to appear engrossed in thought. In April, the petals literally fly off and are causing increasing concern to motorists by attempting one last fling – mating with windscreen wipers.

The purple and green striped pods emit a creaky straining sound, rather like that of forcing rhubarb through a sieve with a slotted metal spoon, but are otherwise insignificant.

Suddenly, and silently, the pods drop their seeds, invariably on the night of the first full moon in May. These "Rye-Ming" seeds are intoxicating to cattle, who can be found lying on their backs in the morning under these trees "cackling". The word "cattle" is a phonetic mutation of "cackle" and not derived from "chattel" as formerly proposed.

Yes, the Poy Tree has a lot to answer for.

Thought Burn pre 1974 *Fallables p.61*

Particles of steel squirt from between forward-heated relentlessly rolling wheels and polished ever-disappearing never-ending parallel track. Hot oil and grease, broadcast from rushing bearings, becomes gelatinously sterile in the cold air and plops dirtily into the granite chips that support the track. Diesel oil is burnt, some of it usefully, to propel the whooshing metal train-animal forward into the world's next molecular moment.

At 80 miles per hour, the sight of passing foliage and man-made monuments gives one a cross-eyed headache and the intense activity within the guts of the animal makes standing or walking persons feel like slightly out of balance gyroscopes.

Soldered into one corner of one of the swaying carriages is a solitary, plain, ordinary, short-hair-cutted man clad in a fairly new dark blue suit which does not quite match his black hair edged with grey or his furry, hairy watch strap. He is hunched over, his elbows fused to his knees and his hands pressed flat against the sides of his head, blinkering his downwards stare from the irreconcilable contrast of ever-changing outside and never-changing inside. Whatever activity he is engaged in, he is certainly calling upon all the normally uncoordinated parts of his being to unite in the task.

Two tiny areas on the randomly spotted vinyl composition floor begin to raise slightly as if marbles are being pushed from underneath. One after the other, the bubbles plop and the rough edges sizzle back just like they're being eaten away by invisible acid. The man's hair mass rocks back and forth on his rigidly stationary head like a wildly excited toupée and is only matched for unusual activity by his furiously trembling eyebrows and the cracked black toe-caps of his shoes moving up and down like wasps' abdomens about to insert their stings. He seems to have at least gained some contact with his thought-penetration circuits and this is confirmed by the smelly fumes of wood smoke and melting plastic that wriggle their way into the atmosphere of the carriage. His eyes, attacked by the fumes, film over with their protective water and the lids are now brought into this canon of electrochemical body counterpoint by the deep-driving need to continue probing for his inside of beyond.

Venetian blinds of furrows ripple down his forehead as his every external body activities mirror all that is going on in his head. Due to the expanded floor hole, the blue-grey atmospheric rubbish is now whooshing, spurting, billowing upwards to conceal the perpetrator of it all, making the carriage a hazy, out of focus, 3-dimensional black and white TV image. His pronounced asthmatic-like breathing, now much louder than the high-pitched roar of the onward-speeding train, is further encouraged by wild elbows pumping in and out from his sides, and the brief sight of an ear that fluctuates between light yellow through red to dark purple signalling through the fog communicates that the moment of knowing the truth of the deep is imminent.

Yes, the final firework show of burnt metal splutters and pops to a gradual halt, the red-hot smoke energy subsides and his searchlight balls of eyes, straining to gain a little bit more open aperture, operate under hydraulic pressure and push downward. His head moves for the first time to follow his eyes and maintain the essential link of communication signals.

He is now seeing the moment of ultimate feedback.

An eruption of hissing spluttery steam, carrying wood and metal splinters and crusty bubbles of burnt floor, violently emits from his thought-crater and covers him in gritty black rubbish, the cruel knowledge flashes through to his spine spring which, uncoiling viciously, bashes his head on the back of the seat.

The train lavatory has just jettisoned its contents!

He staggers and bumps his way to the toilet for a cold wash and rough-up with some semi-absorbent paper towels, all the while discovering and tweeking out small splinters of wood and metal from his face. He eventually slumps back into his seat, his smarting face and aching eyes reminding him of the misled thought journey that took him back round to *before* where he started.

As we leave him, he is blurredly registering clumps and layers of passing foliage, his lower lip moist and hanging out slightly, with an uncomfortable draught agitating up his trouser legs from the hole that was his very own creation.

Thought Pressure 1970 *Fallables p.50*

I carry too much in my head!
 Write it down! Write it down!
 Write it out to read it back, not for publishers to petrify and clog other people's heads with stone thoughts. (That's done this book in!)
 The act of writing thoughts down helps to relieve brain pressure. It also prevents one from churning out the same stuff of conversation over a long period to different people (to use words *at* people) which is using those people as hard reflective surfaces and not, as I feel properly, soft digestive reflective surfaces.

Addition 1974: Churning out the same stuff gives one that sick, ecky feeling in the head and I think in advanced cases is counter-corrected in the head to one of numbed atrophy which is shown in those people who find it impossible to let thought in conversation run fluidly-fluently but must talk tensely about weather, colour of curtains, ailments, grouses.

Too Much For Lunch 1971

Two old chairs sit looking at each other over a carpet of rubbish with wall-decor by British Rail rails and creosoted wooden huts. A silver-birch branch gently swings itself in the breeze of world-thought to replace the stiff-agitation swing of the brittle crumbling chair-occupants' vanished legs. A young lupin dances but a grey-brick house and the occupant's centre hair-parting crack with a crack.

A chestnut tree's leaves and softly erect flower systems wave, inwardly and outwardly, covering all known and unknown feelings.

Two teams, of two boys each, play at throwing jagged stones at each other. One boy, sitting behind a shield which is a small piece of thin wood propped up to a total height of 7", receives a leaping, writhing piece of broken concrete on the knee and his face and body crumple to the dirty-grey ground.

The two bystanding little girls strut forward with great purpose, remove their teddies and cloth rabbits from behind the 7" bit of wood and quickly abandon the aspect – in favour of Sunday lunch.

And so much blossom flashes past my eyes that they hurt so I turn them to distant concrete living-and-dying boxes.

Two Way Site pre 1970   *Fallables p.15*

Flocks of young people at twilight. They're gravitating to a large noisy mechanical crudely-lit fairground. I'm travelling against the flow towards a beautiful sunset with all of the layers and shades of light orange through to deep violet.

War On The Ground pre 1974   *Fallables p.88*

War on the ground is really a man with a large field with curved corrugated huts to keep pigs in to grub all the vegetation off to feed them to get themselves eaten by other men to help those men to have the energy to work to make the curved corrugated metal huts and grow other food in other fields that gets eaten by another lot of men who leave some of it to feed back to the pigs.

Water Play mid 1970s

> The fanatic's freezing dip or cold water plunge.
> The complacent luke-warm soak.
> The happy froth of hot involvement.
> The fervent sweat of steaming heat.
> The suicidal scalding shower, straight from the boiler.

Waters Plumbed 2011/06/22

On my very last live encounter with former friend Roger Waters – 23rd August 1994 – he taught me the first elements of fly-casting in the craft of trout fishing, and we swapped latest CDs. When I got home, I opened his CD case and found – nothing! He had plainly left the CD in his player. So, I could have simply phoned and said, "Look in your player for the CD that should be in this case!" But, being a creative sort of fellow, I made a paper 'CD' on which was a huge enlargement of a fly – you see, I collected flies as a therapy at one point in my life, following on from my general interest in all insects, so I had the right book for the picture. I posted this along with a short letter which contained a poem:

THE DIGITAL TROUT

"Q-sound, O Q-sound!", I shouted all round,
"L. O.! L. O.!" said I, like the fuzz.
But no spatial specialty could B-found –
just a muffly, snuffly, crinkly buzz.

That Waters is no doubt a slippery hound
who's served me his art on a plate –
except that it's paper that's going round and round,
and his trout had the CD as bait.

Oh, silvery splash like a halo of sound,
tell me, Trout, do you fancy a Test?
I'll proffer my box with a fly spinning round
if you leap up and swap for what's best.

After about 3 days of silence, I phoned him and, apart from his accusing me of saying and doing things of which I had no knowledge at all, including my writing a review of his latest work, he had no idea what the poem was about – even though it plainly accompanied the 'CD' artwork. Hindsight now reveals that my presence and presents triggered a shockwave in what is now known to be his paranoia of the period. Two short words from me finished the relationship.

   You might – only 'might', mind you – be right in saying, "Oh, just two nutters swapping dustbin lids for milkbottle tops!"

Plumbed Note 2017/09/21: Actually, the relationship is not finished – just stalled for a while. Creative folk live on different cloud formations – at different levels. Sometimes they might shift clouds, or even float to the ground, but seldom really meet, physically or ethereally.

Whirls Of Brain *[read on the John Peel BBC 'Night Ride' programme, 1968/08/14]*

As I sit here in whirls of brain and pounds of heart –
                                                            "Which part?"
As I reflect upon the conditions of the emotions of some humans, and the non-emotions of an awful lot of others –
                                           "What happens? Which humans?"
A few precious friends get even more precious – and things disappear in ever-decreasing circles. But then things brighten and people ask questions and I ask questions and statements get made and opposition is overthrown! – and it's really very difficult to answer silly questions, but they've got to be answered, or the people get sillier.

Xmas Croppers – From Crackers pre 1974 *Fallables p.66*

1. "How do you punch a hole in a hole?"

> You don't, but building fresh matter round it
> might cause it to drop right through
> into the down-ness of spacial alti-librium."

2. "How do you see in the dark?"
> "By eating lots of carrots!"

"No, no, they're only good for peeing in a park."
> "All right, how do you see in the dark?"

"By creating enough luminescent brain energy
that your eyes turn into searchlights!"

Youthful Optimism pre 1970 *Fallables p.97*

Yes, you see, I saw a lot of miserable people on the tube train one day and said:
> "Get your peg in the right hole, missus,
> before you chip off the corners –
> and possibly even lay bare your embarrassment."

which caused them to be no better, it would seem, but I'm only young now so maybe something will happen later.

Youths pre 1970 *Fallables p.16*

> Youths wandered lonely in a crowd
> with golden-shoe-stepped little girls
> for all the purpose in the world.

titles index

10p Travel Fare	135	Avant garde 1	17	**C**	
		Avant garde 2	17	C.L.F.	21
A				Calculated Lateness	
A Bit Of Paper	56	**B**		Factor (C.L.F.)	21
A Brisk Walk Out	102	Back Britain	104	Cards Thankyou	107
A Great Deal Of Mouth	56	Backstage	18	Care	21
A Pleasant Scene	57	Bag Of Love	104	Challenge	21
A Revelous Fellow	102	Banjo	18	Chrisfarce	108
A Twisted Tree	102	Barbed Wire	61	Circular Frustration	145
A Useful Brick	58	Bath Oil Thankyou	105	Clown	21
Abuse	58	Bathwomb	18	Collaboration	21
Academia	14	BBC fees	18	Comfort	22
Academic	14	Beer Posture	143	Communication	22
Academics & artists	14	Belief	18	Composer	22
Acceleration and		Below Bungalow	143	Composers	22
intensification	14	Bifurcated- Half		Composition	22
Add Minister	58	Truncated	144	Conceived	145
Advice	15	Bit Of Paper, A	56	Confession	110
Ailments	60	Bitter Letters	62	Confidence	22
Alcoholic Intake	142	Blackbird	18	Conflict	22
Allegiance	15	Blame	18	Conscious analysis	23
Almost Nearly	103	Blessing Of Art Craft	144	Consciousness	23
Alphabite	60	Bloomers	62	Conservation Piece	64
Analytic	15	Board	19	Conspicuousness	23
Anonymity	15	Body	19	Control 1	23
Another Night		Bon Fire	105	Control 2	23
Thought	142	Bother	19	Convention	23
Anxiety	15	Bow-Tie Thankyou	105	Cook life	24
Apology	15	Boxes	19	Cookbook	23
Appearances	61	Brain 1	19	Cooking Roast Pork,	
Apples	16	Brain 2	19	Braised Onions &	
Application	16	Brain Slivers	145	Fresh Runner Beans –	
Art 1	16	Brain-Twirl	106	With A Bottle Of Red	
Art 2	16	Brass Butterfly	62	Wine – For The	
Art 3	16	Brisk Walk Out, A	102	Cook And Author (the	
Art 4	16	Britain Is Great	107	same), On	128
Art 5	16	British Wail	63	Council	24
Art 6	17	Building	19	Critics	24
Art 7	17	Burn	19	Crying	24
Artist	17	Business	20	Cubicle	65
Assessment	17	By The Sea	107	Cynicism	24

D

Dance	65
Depression 1	25
Depression 2	25
Depression 3	25
Depression 4	25
Depression 5	25
Dinner Party	65
Disgust	25
Doctor's waiting	25
Dog-Walk	66
Doors	110
Dream	26
Dribblings	26
Drugs	26, 66

E

Eccentricity	27
Elastic bands	27
Emerging From A Walk-Way Tunnel To Wait For Tube Train, On	158
En-devour	27
Energy	27
Enthusiasm	27, 66
Environment	146
Equipment 1	28
Equipment 2	28
Exclamation Sideways	146
Expert Docking In Newcastle	147

F

Failure	66
Fanaticism	29
Farce	29
Fashion	110
Fashion 1	29
Fashion 2	29
Fashion 3	29
Fear	29
Fear The Lord	67
Film	111
Finish	29
For Katie Hewitt – aged 9	112
For Sale	112
Friend	30
Friend Relations	151
Friends	30
Future	30

G

Geesin's An Odd Name	113
German Forest, In A	153
Give	68
Glasgow – an aspect	68
God	31, 69
God-slogans perceived	31
God Speaks	31
Golf	31
Gone – But Nearly There	114
Good	32
Grand Search	70
Grated Britain	116
Great Deal Of Mouth, A	56
Group Dressing Room, In	154

H

Hard/Soft	33
Head Boil	71
Head-Knock	72
Heart	72
Heat	151
Help	33
Holes	72
Holidays	33
Houses	117
Human 1	33
Human 2	33
Human Development	33

I

I Dream Of Life	151
Ideas In Trees	152
In A German Forest	153
Individuality	34
Infatuation	34
In Group Dressing Room	154
Initiation	154
Intention	34
I've Never Come This Way Before	118

J

Jane & Mike Fond Do	120
Jazz Band	73
Jesus	74

K

Katie Hewitt- aged 9, For	112
Knock Down – Stand Up	156
Knowledge 1	35
Knowledge 2	35
Knowledge 3	35

L

Late	36
Law Profession	36
Life 1	36
Life 2	36
Life 3	36
Lifelaw	36
Litter Dropping	156
Living Too Close	157
Lockdown	121
Loneliness	37
Look	74
Lost And Found	74
Love	37
Lying In Bed	121

M

Machines	38, 157
Mad	38
Man Of Business	122
March Of Time	157
Marks	39
Material Miss	75
Matter	39
Media	39
Message	124
Mini Liquid Golf Game Thankyou	124

Molecular Structure	158	
Money	39	
Monks Green Farm (An Imaginary History)	125	
Movement	39	

N

Needle	40
Negro Girls	40
Nerves	40, 75
Nervous Exhaustion	40
New Couple, To A	138
Newspapers	40
Nice Old Lady	125
Night Of Nights, The	86
No Doubt Influenced By Spike Milligan	126
Nourishment	40
Now – more or less	75
Nut	76
Nutcracker Thankyou	127

O

O.T.T.	41
O'er Precipice	127
On Cooking Roast Pork, Braised Onions & Fresh Runner Beans – With A Bottle Of Red Wine – For The Cook And Author (the same)	128
On Emerging From A Walk-Way Tunnel To Wait For Tube Train	158
On Going	77
On Visiting A Middle-Class Aspect	128
One Pair Of Eyes	129
Opening For Closing	159
Opening for going through	41
Openings	41
Oriental Food Thankyou	129
Our Dance	160
Outlets	41
Outrage	41
Overload	41

P

Pace	42
Page Watcher	130
Passion	42
Past	42
Patterned Hankies Thankyou	131
Pear-Shaped Man, The	137
Pen, The	137
Penny	42
Perception	78
Perfection	42
Performance	42
Performance Aspects	43
Performance – Bracknell, 25th May 1979	78
Perversity	43
Pets	43
Philosophy 1	43
Philosophy 2	43
Phone	161
Platform	43
Pleasant Scene, A	57
Politicians	43
Poster Defacing	161
Postman Carried A Large Tree, The	88
Poy Tree, The	167
Present-Future	44
Pretty Little Faces	79
Pretty Little Girls	80
Problem	44
Profession	44
Professional	44
Progress	44
Protection	44
Proverbs	44

R

Rabbit	45
Railway Sleepers	162
Rainbow Bit	45
Relief	131
Religion	45
Reply To "Chordless Electric Drill" Newspaper Ad. Sent By Ian Breakwell From Ireland	162
Return	163
Revelous Fellow, A	102
Rise Up Sebastian!	81
Robbery	45
Ron's Address	132
Round And Round	83
Rules (real)	45

S

Sam Smith, To	139
School Groups – 8.55am	84
Science of thought	46
Scraped Youth	163
Search Light For Quality	164
Searching	165
See Straight	46
Seen	84
Self Note	166
Sensation	46
Sentence	85
Sharp Saddle	166
Shift	46
Shipping Water	85
Shortbread Thankyou	133
Shoulders (round)	46
Shyness	46
Sick	46
Sincerity	47
Smoking 1	47
Smoking 2	47
Solution	47
Sound	166
Sound, The	89
Space Notion	47
Spider's Life	166
Splashback	47
Standards	47
Standing Joke	133

Statement made before knowing how to work properly	48	Timidity	50	Virus	52
		Tiredness	50	Visiting A Middle-Class Aspect, On	128
		To A New Couple	138		
Stillness	48	To Be Again Forthcoming With The Second And Third The Next	93	**W**	
Stimulation	48			Waiting For Life	98
Suicide 1	48			Walking	99
Suicide 2	48			Wallpaper	53
Suicide 3	48	To Sam Smith	139	War	53
Sun	48	To The Sterile Village Of Bothwell, Lanarkshire	94	War On The Ground	170
Superiority	49			Water Play	170
Surprise	49	Today	95	Waters Plumbed	170
		Too Much For Lunch	169	Wattage	53
T		Toothbrush	51	Waves	53
Talking 1	50	Train Travellers	51, 96	Well-Appointed Roll, The	138
Talking 2	50	Travel-theory	51		
Talking Man	85	Tree	51	Whirls Of Brain	171
Tartan	134	Turmoil	96	Widdle	99
Technology	50	Twist	96	Wind Of Life	100
The Night Of Nights	86	Twisted Tree, A	102	Work-party	53
The Pear-Shaped Man	137	Two Bottles Bordeaux Thankyou	140	World Problems	53
The Pen	137			World View	53
The Postman Carried A Large Tree	88	Two Feet And A Mouth	97	Wrong Line	101
		Two Fellows	140		
The Poy Tree	167	Two Way Site	170	**X**	
The Sound	89	Two ways – at least	51	Xmas Croppers – From Crackers	172
The Well-Appointed Roll	138	**U**			
Thought Burn	167	Unbuilding	141		
Thought Pressure	169	Universe	52	**Y**	
Thought Spot	91	Useful Brick, A	58	Young and Old	54
Thought Weave	92			Youthful Optimism	172
Time 1	50	**V**		Youths	172
Time 2	50	Valentines	141